THE HUMILITY OF BEING FOUND

Rescue!

Galatians 1:1-4

THE HUMILITY OF BEING FOUND

A Journey to Rescue

Kevin B. Cain

ELM HILL

A Division of
HarperCollins Christian Publishing

www.elmhillbooks.com

© 2019 Kevin B. Cain

The Humility of Being Found

A Journey to Rescue

Published in Nashville, Tennessee, by Elm Hill, an imprint of Thomas Nelson. Elm Hill and Thomas Nelson are registered trademarks of HarperCollins Christian Publishing, Inc.

Elm Hill titles may be purchased in bulk for educational, business, fund-raising, or sales promotional use. For information, please e-mail SpecialMarkets@ ThomasNelson.com.

Scripture quotations marked NASB are from New American Standard Bible˚. Copyright © 1960, 1962, 1963, 1968, 1971, 1972, 1973, 1975, 1977, 1995 by The Lockman Foundation. Used by permission. (www.Lockman.org)

Scripture quotations marked THE MESSAGE are from The Message. Copyright © by Eugene H. Peterson 1993, 1994, 1995, 1996, 2000, 2001, 2002. Used by permission of NavPress. All rights reserved. Represented by Tyndale House Publishers, Inc.

Library of Congress Cataloging-in-Publication Data

Library of Congress Control Number: 2019912953

ISBN 978-1-400328499 (Paperback)
ISBN 978-1-400328505 (eBook)

FOR GRANNY

There was always a book, an encouragement to read, and a calling to meet with the One Who rescues us.

THE COVER

The pictures on the cover are from my personal journal. During a 2015 autumn trip to Seattle, my wife, oldest son, and I visited the city's iconic Public Market Center. There, amidst flying salmon, the diversity of other food offerings, flowers, and art, we stumbled upon a woman selling journals covered with natural animal hides and filled with journal pages of recycled, imperfect paper. I wanted one, but in my wife's eyes I could see an immediate-future Christmas present she desired to purchase for me, so I never reached for my wallet. Instead, we took the woman's business card, and within a month and a few days, one of the journals was under our family Christmas tree as one of my Christmas presents. The morning after the journal's unwrapping, I began putting pen to the unrefined pages. I was preparing for my first sermon series of the year titled, "This Day's Bread." It was to be an exploration into the individual's association with the body and blood of Christ. As I began to record eucharistic scriptures, I discovered a raised image at the bottom of the journal page upon which I was writing. I ran my fingers over it. There waiting on me was a resemblance of Jesus' beaten, but unbroken body hanging on the cross. In black ink, I started to outline the perfection housed in the invisible image rising from the flawed paper. With the likeness defined, I sketched a cross, and there was my Rescuer, your Rescuer, our Rescuer—this One we each so often fight against, saying, "Humble yourself and be found." In Jesus' perfect rescue of each of us, we find our desired rescue.

—K.B.C.

"I'm God commissioned. So I greet you with the great words, grace and peace! We know the meaning of those words because Jesus Christ rescued us from this evil world we're in by offering himself as a sacrifice for our sins. God's plan is that we all experience that rescue."

—GALATIANS 1:1–4 THE MESSAGE

CONTENTS

Rest and Peace –
A Poem of Rescue

"Rest for my soul and peace for my mind," I cried.
But neither came.
There was no rest.
There was no peace.
Neither came.

Too much clutter.
Too much speed.
Too much noise.
Too many people.
I loved the too much,
Far too much.
And so I cried,
"Rest for my soul and peace for my mind!"
But neither came.
There was no rest.
There was no peace.
Neither came.

"I don't know."
Silence.

"I think I'm dying."
I longed for transformation and labored to sleep,
But dedication to conformity outlaws the compassionate
worthiness of rest.
Rest never comes to those who are too *too* to respect her.
"It's over," she said.
"It's going to be okay," he said.
I surrendered to the defeat and started the pilgrimage to
victory.

Victory ...
There is humbled laughter.

In loneliness, I did not yet know of solitude's existence.
I heard her footsteps.
Breath that I no longer worried from where it would come
returned to me.
Not healthy,
I knew I was fine.

The God I had always loved;
The God I had always spoken to;
The God Who closed my eyes;
The God Whose name I declared to the lost,
Found me hiding under myself,
And loved me,
Rescued me.

"Thank You."
"Thank You for him."
"Thank You for her."
Rest and peace.

—KBC

ROYA'S STEM AND LEAF

Roya's Stem and Leaf

I was born in Westover, West Virginia, population 4,182. She was born in Tehran, Iran, population 8.3 million.

She is Roya, my sister-in-law, one who reflects the face of God more vividly than most I know. Roya is married to my brother. How Nick is my brother is a testimony for another time. It is certainly a tale worthy of being told.

We had not been to Nick and Roya's home for a few years. There was no avoidance, and we had excusable excuses, but when it comes to time with those you love, substantive moments together should really be prioritized, rather than excused away.

Nick has far more vigor than I, so at 9:45 p.m. my brother wanted to make up for lost time. He said, "Everyone load up. We're going bowling." Their son and my sons grabbed their coats, and, along with the boys, my equally zestful wife bolted toward the already running SUV, but neither Roya nor I made a single move. They were all ready to head out to knock down some pins. Roya and I were content to stay put and talk. Both sides respected the other. The garage door closed, and they were on their way. Roya and I settled in.

"Would you like tea, Kevin?"

"Thank you, Roya. I *would* like some."

There are few things better than Iranian tea, especially when it is paired with Roya's sweet soul. Tea with Roya is one of the exceeding, abundant, above all I can ever ask or think preliminary tastes of heaven God has stationed in this world. It is nice to know prayerful portions of "on earth as it is in heaven" are already being realized.

Roya served the tea, we began to stoke the conversation with the necessary preliminary particulars of life's catching-up inventory, but in a very short time, our chitchat began to sound spiritually deep waters. Like Jesus' keen ability to educate with the streams of parable, in spiritual overflow, Roya and I immersed ourselves.

Roya said, "May I share with you an Iranian parable?"

"Of course," I said.

In her elegant accent and surrendering to technological modernity, Roya said, "It is presented on a YouTube video with captioning in Farsi. I will have to translate."

Roya called up the video on her iPhone and began.

There was once a community of insects living just below the waterline of a dark and murky pond. They had lived there for years. As a matter of fact, generation upon generation of this community of insects had resided in the environment so that no one ever believed there was any other existence beyond their borders of stagnation.

After many years, into the community, a new insect was born. He was of the same nature, the same nurture, and he was bound by the same atmosphere. There was nothing different about this one, except that he always seemed to keep his gaze upward. The fellow insects of this dreary liquid world called the young insect to lower his eyes, but something above kept drawing his attention.

One day, the leader of the community said to him, "Why do you always look toward our great kingdom's ceiling?"

The young insect's answer was simple. He said, "If you look up, you can clearly see there is something above the dismal waters of our country. Don't you see? There is light and greater life on the horizon of this darkness."

The entire community came to an immediate shriek of silence. The leader of the community said to the young insect, "Don't you ever say that again! There is no horizon and nothing beyond the waters that keeps us. If we leave the cradle of fluid we have always known, then we will die. Now stop this reckless dreaming, lower your eyes, and exist as we have always existed."

Everyone concurred, and, after his scolding, the young insect held in silence, but deep inside he knew he was right. Then and there, he made a vow to himself. While everyone was watching he would live in the watery haze with his eyes straight ahead, but when no one was looking, he would look up with the hope of finding a way to be rescued from his dead sea home; to find a ladder-of-sorts to rise and live in the light he was certain was waiting at the horizon he had been commanded to deny.

For some time, life went on just like this. Head down, he made his way through the darkness, but he always seized the private seconds to look toward the welcoming light. Then one day, there it was: a leaf from above had pierced the watery ceiling with its stem calling to every insect to ascend from their liquid coffin and up to resurrected life.

"Everyone," the young insect cried. "We've been rescued. See! A leaf's stem has come to our world. All we have to do is go up the stem and into the life above."

The leader of the insects and all the community with him said, "Never! Stay away from the stem. It's not part of our world. If you go up that stem to the end of our waters, you will be cast out of our kingdom forever."

The young insect said, "I cannot live in this darkness any longer. It's not true life. I have to go up the stem. All that is true is waiting there for me and all of you too."

With shaming accusation, all the other insects turned away from him. Nervous and excited, the young insect was left alone to travel up this lone stem that had entered his world. The young insect exhaled every bit of his kingdom's remaining water, closed his eyes, and ventured up the stem and through the limits of the only life he'd ever known. Opening one eye to a squint, he found himself on the stem's stable leaf, and surrounding him was an even greater world than he had imagined. Looking down, he could still see the movement of the dark, watery kingdom below, but, as a result of the gracious appearance of the stem coupled with his own faithfulness, the young insect was free from his previous world of death.

Then a miraculous thing happened. In an instant, the young insect was newly created into the most glorious creature he could have ever imagined. It was as though he had been filled with a new breath. All around him, he saw distinct creatures he did not know, but, somehow, he loved these creatures purely and completely. Like him, they too had ventured up the stem and onto the leaf. Like him, they too were equally, individually transformed forever.

The video ended.

"Isn't that a beautiful parable, Kevin?"

"It is, Roya. This parable of stem and leaf is who I have come to know the Messiah to be. Through stem and leaf, all humanity can be rescued."

With parable alive before us, silently, contentedly, Roya and I finished our tea.

FIGHTING AGAINST OUR RESCUER

FIGHTING AGAINST
OUR RESCUER

During the first week of June 1984, I and two other teenage boys were drowning during a swimming pool rescue gone horribly wrong.

It was the end of my seventh-grade year at Westover Junior High School. My sister, Keely—two years older—was celebrating her class's *Ninth Grade Skip Day* at our family's home and in our family's in-ground pool with her classmates, located a mere 500 yards from Westover Junior High School.

One day prior to the turn in of my sister and her fellow junior high graduates' pencils and books, they celebrated their *Skip Day*, so that educational authority would hear their shouts of teenage rebellion. W.J.H.S's annual tradition of mostly innocuous, non-violent protest always earned one final bushel of teachers' dirty looks. Unfortunately, and in the spirit of the not-so-famous Paul Jacob's song, I was a seventh grade, running-dog lackey of the ninth-grade bourgeoisie. Denied access, I had been relegated to the doldrums of school while, at the same time, wrapped in the loving arms of my parents' shiny new pool, thirty or so privileged fourteen-year-olds were practicing their cannonballs.

The 2:30 afternoon bell rang.

I ran to my locker, spun the combination, pulled the latch, grabbed my stuff, slammed the locker door, burst from the school, and ran the short distance from our junior high to my parents' front door. Gliding up the stairs to my bedroom, I then put on my swimming trunks and headed out to the pool. I knew I would be unwelcome to my sister and her bullying girlfriends, but the guys tolerated me, so my plan was to head straight to the diving board line and ignore Keely's cries of, "Mom!!! Make Kevin go inside!!! No one wants him out here!!! He's ruining everything!!!" I would be safe. Mom was always within eyeshot of the pool, but this day our mother offered a brief extension of grown-up freedom to Keely and her friends, and to me grace, in the form of my mother's momentary turned-deaf ear.

Just like I described it, I headed to the diving board line, the guys welcomed me, and Keely, with relatively certain violent threats, screamed her disapproval of my entire presence. I paid her no mind. I waited my turn, stepped to the board, ran to the end, jumped, and in aquatic lock-step with the divers before me, I watched for the football being thrown in my descending direction by the Westover Junior High School Terriers' departing varsity quarterback.

I caught it.

Still immersed in the water and with the ball nestled securely under my arm, I prayed, "Thank You, Lord!"

With the benefit of cover by the approving males, I swam to the deep-end ladder to exit the pool, rather than the shallow-end steps where my sister and her fight club female counterparts were ready and waiting to pummel me. Safely back to the diving board line, I stood behind a kid named Curly Dixon. He was a ninth-grader, but, while two years my senior, we had been good buddies prior to either of us being in kindergarten. I was safe with Curly.

The next young man jumped, and he registered an incompletion. Mostly internally, but a bit externally, I beamed. I had caught the same tight spiral this upperclassman had just missed. I was quite proud of myself and knew I had earned the privilege of at least one dropped pass, before I ran the risk of being kicked out of the security of the diving board line. In the midst of my gloating, the football floated to the pool's deep-end edge.

"I'll get it," said a completely dry, cut-off-jean-shorts-instead-of-trunks-wearing young man named Chris Luckey. No one thought a thing of Chris Luckey bending over the edge of the deep-end to retrieve the football, but there was good reason for Chris Luckey being completely dry. Chris Luckey had been an all-day *Ninth Grade Skip Day* pool party attendee, but Chris Luckey could not swim. Until the moment when Chris Luckey instinctively leapt to retrieve the football, Christ Luckey hadn't been ten feet from even the shallow end.

Chris reached for the pigskin, lost his balance, and fell straight into eight feet deep of water.

Everyone knew this was no joke. Chris was drowning. I don't know why *we* did it, and I don't know why among all those kids *we* were the only two who moved, but Curly and I jumped straight in the water to save Chris. I dove to one side, and Curly dove to the other. Underwater, we flanked Chris as we attempted to get him to the surface.

Sadly, we were failing. In our attempt to get Chris above the water line, Curly and I were deep under water and trying with all our strength to push Chris up and out. We were quickly exhausting the last bits of the panicked breaths we had gasped prior to crashing through the surface of the deep end. With his own head still under water, Chris, in his attempt to rise to the surface, pushed Curly and me down deeper.

Chris, in his panic, fought against the ones who dove in to save him.

Resistance was digging our three impending watery graves.

In *A Grief Observed*, C.S. Lewis writes:

Meanwhile, where is God? This is one of the most disquieting symptoms. When you are happy, so happy that you have no sense of needing Him, so happy that you are tempted to feel His claims upon you as an interruption, if you remember yourself and turn to Him with gratitude and praise, you will be—or so it feels—welcomed with open arms. But go to Him when your need is desperate, when all other help is vain, and what do you find? A door slammed in your face, and a sound of bolting and double bolting on the inside. After that, silence. You may as well turn away. The longer you wait, the more emphatic the silence will become. There are no lights in the windows. It might be an empty house. Was it ever inhabited? It seemed so once. And that seeming was as strong as this. What can this mean? Why is He so present a commander in our time of prosperity and so very absent a help in time of trouble?

... The time when there is nothing at all in your soul except a cry for help may be just the time when God can't give it: you are like the drowning man who can't be helped because he clutches and grabs. Perhaps your own reiterated cries deafen you to the voice you hoped to hear.

On the other hand, "Knock and it shall be opened." But does knocking mean hammering and kicking the door like a maniac? And there's also "To him that hath shall be given." After all, you must have a capacity to receive, or even omnipotence can't give. Perhaps your own passion temporarily destroys the capacity.

It doesn't matter whether it is two boys attempting to save one boy from drowning in a neighborhood pool, or a brokenhearted brother-in-Christ mourning the loss of his wife, or a person shackled by spiritual death, thievery, and destruction. The Messiah, motivated by God's love, dove into this world, beyond, and back again to rescue all of us. The Rescuer has journeyed to rescue us, and, in each journey to be rescued, each must stop fighting against this One Who rescues.

Chris and Curly both gave me permission to tell you this story.

THE HUMILITY OF BEING FOUND

The Humility of Being Found

*T**he humility of being found.*

These are the words a Jesuit priest spoke to me while I was attending a silent retreat adjacent to Lake Winnebago in Oshkosh, Wisconsin.

Father Gillick is blind, but he saw me like no other person ever has. My life has been completely different since that moment. All my life I have done my very best to be good, to keep the rules, to measure up, to never disappoint. To choke down my tears when I really just wanted to cry. Cry in such a way that tears were streaming down my face, dripping from my chin, and I didn't even care. The world would simply have to deal with my tears. I wanted to hide no more.

But I never did. I was far too afraid to disappoint.

To pastor is to remain on your horse and die because the world would rather you stay there and masquerade your pain, your disappointments, your grief, and a thousand other things, than come down and admit who you really are. Because if you come down, then there must be an admission. You are just like one of them. God doesn't hear you in a greater way than He hears them. You aren't special. You are common, but in your commonality you are committed; and, your commitment is to do your very best to help Jesus carry the burdens of the world. A task that really isn't yours.

It was March of 2017, and since 2004 and my nervous breakdown— *did he just say that?*—nothing much had changed. I learned how to more proficiently choke down tears I so wanted to cry. I had more tools for my toolbox and had re-framed the picture of my life, but eggshells were still the ground upon which I walked ... and I was getting very tired.

The previous November, one of my dear friends, whose name is Jason, leaned over on the couch in my office and said, "You wanna go on a silent retreat with me and some of my friends next year?" I didn't even know what a silent retreat was, but I wanted to go. My world was too crowded, too noisy, and far too fast. I couldn't manage the whole world, nor could I manage the perimeter of my own existence.

We return to March of 2017.

I flew to Milwaukee, Wisconsin. I waited at the curb for people I really didn't even know, but they were calling me, *brother.*

Honestly, I thought they were just making fun of me like I believed everyone else had for so many years. It was a lampoon, and I was their fool. I couldn't even imagine people I had never met could be so kind, so genuine ... but they were. Jason picked me up and let me sit up front. Immediately, Jason began introducing me to our fellow Silent Retreat retreatants.

Andrew: He just kept smiling in my direction. The eyes truly are the light of the soul.

Lambert: He didn't know me, and he lived on the other side of the world, but somehow he saw the darkness crying to come out of my heart and said, "I thought I was bringing this book for me, but I can see I have brought it for you."

Ben: He was so kind.

Pat: He sat next to me and put his arm around me.

Could I trust their genuineness?

Jay showed us around the Jesuit Retreat Center and walked us down a back hallway. He said, in his Jason-kind of way, "You each need to sign up to talk to Father Gillick. He's amazing. Your lives will never be the same again." I honestly don't even know if that's what Jason said, but that's what I want to believe he said. I immediately, along with all the other Oshkosh, silent retreat pilgrims, signed up for fifteen minutes with Father Larry Gillick. I had no clue what I was signing up for, but it just seemed right.

He walked into the upstairs conference room that night, banged his head on the wall sconce, did not even acknowledge it, then sat down, opened his braille bible, and said, "Things take the time they take. You don't need to worry."

That weekend I took more than a hundred pages of notes, doing my very best to chronicle each and every one of Father Gillick's words. They were wisdom. I wanted them. I needed them.

Then came my fifteen minutes. We did not talk about sports, nor did we talk about weather. He did say, though, he knew of Wheeling Jesuit University, where my wife played college basketball and received her physical therapy degree.

I missed her so much. "What am I doing in Oshkosh, Wisconsin?!?!" Every other town, at every other time when I was away from home, I asked that same question, and I ran. This time though, I stayed. I was so afraid. I was all alone. I had to be absolutely silent. But I stayed. I didn't run.

The small talk ended.

The fifteen minutes were over.

Tears were streaming down my face, but I had conditioned myself for forty-six years to cry without a sound. There was no way this gray-haired, sweater-wearing priest without physical sight could look into *my soul* and see the tears pouring down *my cheeks.*

Father Gillick, as a priest of a holy nation I knew of but had never seen, leaned from his chair toward me in mine.

Without sight, he looked with his holy vision into my eyes and set me free. "Kevin," he said, "big boys do cry."

He knew. I didn't know how, but he knew. He saw my tears. He saw my hurt. He saw all my years of embarrassment, and masquerade, and hiding, and fear, and shame, and belief that I never measured up. He saw my mask of prose and my heart of poetry. He saw it all and told me with those blind eyes and nary a word, "God sees you, and God loves you just as you are."

Then with words, Father Gillick said, "The humility of being found."

My fifteen minutes were up.

I left. I have never spoken to Father Gillick again. My life has been changed forever.

No, the only thing I want for this world's people is to be free from this world's rhythms. God has perfectly authored every single day for each person when, as Psalm 139 says, there was not yet one of them. I don't want people to be held by their hurt, but held by joy within all that pain, and, frankly, all that pleasure. I want to live, and I want people to live, and not simply exist. Death is dead, and Jesus has called us to live in the land of the living. There truly are some among us who will never taste death.

Humility is required to be found.

You can continue to cover up all that pain, but you will never be found until you allow your tears to stream and your nose to run. God is speaking to you right now saying, "I see your pain, your hurt, your fears, your covering up, and I have said to it, 'This far you may come, but no farther. Here your proud waves must stop.'"

In order to be found, you must be humble.

I must be humble.

The Messiah has pierced our world.

He wants so badly to rescue each of us, so we must stop fighting against His loving, rescuing arms.

We must rest in humility and be found.

It is in His journey from Upper Room—*"Let not your hearts be troubled, neither be afraid ..."*—to Gethsemane—*"Put your swords away"*—to a Good Friday that was not so good—*"Father forgive them ... It is finished!"*—to Saturday's wait ... to Sunday's declaration of realized life and life more abundant, that each of us will encounter our rescue.

> *The God I had always loved;*
> *The God I had always spoken to;*
> *The God Who closed my eyes;*
> *The God Whose name I declared to the lost,*
> *Found me hiding under myself,*
> *And loved me,*
> *Rescued me.*

The humility of being found.

A Good Friday Calling
to Rescue

A Good Friday Calling
to Rescue

I was ten years old when I realized Jesus' death, burial, and resurrection is humanity's means of spiritual rescue.

In our little United Methodist Church, in our Nazareth of West Virginia, suitably named, Westover, my brotherhood with Jesus began with a sermon by a substitute preacher. This pastor of another UM church traveled west over the Monongahela River, and, with our less-than-a-hundred member congregation, he shared a message focusing on Jesus' reconciling death, burial, and resurrection. Only a decade deep into life, church was my rhythm, but this particular Sunday, for whatever reason, it all became real. I knew the messianic mantra, but as this man who had exchanged his pulpit with our preacher spoke of God's Son bridging the chasm between death and life, I knew I needed to take an actual spiritual step, rather than go on dancing the two-step of religious conceptualism. While I didn't journey on my Via Dolorosa that morning, within weeks, a revivalist visited our local church, preached a similar message, and I began a life-long waltz with the Savior. As Christians say it: *I gave my life to Christ.*

I know quick, convenient answers will come, but what does it mean to *give one's life to Christ?*

I have a better answer to the question now, than I did then, but soon after my revival meeting conversion, I spent the night at my best pal's house and told his mother about my born-again experience. She was a woman who always made the two of us stand back-to-back to see who was taller, believing whoever *was taller* was ahead on the scoreboard of some sort of life competition I never really understood. Regardless, I loved my friend and his family very much—I still do—and she also knew every word of *The Old Rugged Cross*, so with my love and her knowledge of the Cokesbury hymnal, I was content to be transparent. She questioned me with more love than legalism. My testimony held strong, and in that moment, there was realization that I acknowledged Him before humanity (Somewhere along the way in my Christian indoctrination, I had heard Rev. Billy Graham say we had to acknowledge Jesus before men, or Jesus wouldn't acknowledge us before His Father in Heaven, so acknowledgment of the Savior was at the top of my ten-year-old priority list).

Since that night at my buddy's house, I have spoken of my testimony many more times, and while some have reminded me over the years I speak of my *aha Immanuel moment* too much, my once-was-blind-but-now-I-see submission conversation with Christ is still one of my most favorite stories to tell.

As my teens were crossing into my twenties, I sensed the gospel could no more be confined to a Roman cross than it could an Easter Sunday morning. So, during the last week of Lent, I attended Maundy Thursday Holy Communion, and for the first time, I attended my local assembly's Good Friday service.

During Thursday's Holy Communion service, there was movement, and singing, and kneeling, and reception of the sacrament. Yet, on Good Friday, everyone and everything was quiet ... too quiet. The silence rattled me. The Passion narrative was read, the sanctuary was stripped, one candle burned, and then, in silence, we all left. Some began talking again as they reached their cars which were parked alongside mine in the volunteer fire department parking lot, but my silence carried me about a mile away to Westover Park. It was raining, and something seemed to be telling me the rain was more than appropriate.

While there is no mention of rain on the day Jesus died to rescue creation, I cannot imagine there was only a noontime darkness blocking out the sunlight. Storm clouds must have brought an additional ebony to the already-present darkness of both evil and good. Rain was the river of creation that ran between the two shores of shadows, demonic and divine. So, there on my personal Golgotha, I stood without an umbrella, attempting to join with my crucified Christ as I willingly welcomed pain's precipitation. I could not get silence out of my head nor conviction from my heart. Both were held necessarily in place, and I, without condemnation, was being perfectly embraced by the Messiah and His refusal to come down. In the rain, without presumptuous vow, I committed to keeping a Holy Week vigil forever.

A few years later, I heard a pastor speak these words: *You cannot fully experience the resurrection until you experience the crucifixion.* Christ's journey was His own, but I wanted to do my best to walk with Him. The candlelight of the Upper Room is minimal, and Gethsemane's garden is only touched by moonlight, but my committed-to-vigil was gaining greater clarity. As treelike men walk about, I could somewhat see the formation of a thirty-six-hour intercessory prayer, worship, and contemplative journey from the Upper Room to Holy Saturday morning.

Those first-century followers had headed to the Upper Room thinking it was any other Passover night, but within seconds, or minutes, or hours, their hearts became troubled as they realized they would not be drinking any more wine with Jesus their Rabbi, until they were drinking it in heaven with Jesus, their resurrected Messiah. In actuality, they did not even know what drinking in heaven meant because, until sometime on Sunday evening, Jesus remained simply their Rabbi, alive, or dead, or stolen, or resurrected, or something.

For the disciples it was dark, and silent, and rainy from the Upper Room, to the Garden, to the striking of the Shepherd and the sheep scattering, to the night, to their respective places of hiding, to a high priest's courtyard, to an enemy's fire of hot coals, to the darkness of denial, to thirty pieces of silver thrown back and a euthanizing rope and tree, to the shadow of those crying, "Crucify," to Barabbas' inky breath of false freedom, to a hill seen by everyone that no one seemed to see, to an unwelcome shade foreign to noontime, to three, to a request before Pilate, to the dusk of a borrowed tomb, to the longest of nights wondering if there ever were going to be another dawn. Then there was dawn, and the dawn left them all wondering if the gloom of their grief would cease. At least they had Sunday when the Body would be properly prepared.

These were my thoughts for many years. Many years, until I had a local assembly of my own where the prayer closet of Maundy Thursday and Good Friday could be celebrated in the form of a thirty-six-hour prayer vigil.

Much trial and error occurred from birth as a new church-planting pastor at twenty-eight years old to forty years old as an established, founding pastor of a planted church. Still, my age being forty years old and twelve years as a local assembly within our community seemed to be the moment where the Holy Week vigil was to be appropriately launched. That first night of Thirty-Six Hours of Prayer I journaled these words:

April 21, 2011   *Maundy Thursday 9:00 p.m.*

What is longer, forty days without food or thirty-six hours of prayer? Such is the question before me. I have just finished listening to Matthew 26:36–46 which chronicles the spirit's willingness and the flesh's weakness in Gethsemane. The enemy is already whispering condemnation and failure in my ear.

Jesus' words in the Sermon on the Mount are true though. "Do not worry about tomorrow. Tomorrow has enough to worry for itself. Sufficient for the day is its own trouble."

I press on.

I am reminded of my first real experience with Maundy Thursday and Good Friday. Silence overwhelmed me. I truly considered, for the first time, not just the crucifixion of Jesus but the agony, ridicule, hatred, and loneliness that stands as the clothing of the crucifixion. I remember going to

Westover Park in the rain and just looking into the expanse of beauty think-
ing that He did that to rescue me.

I never want to minimize that reality.

It is easy to sleep while others bleed and agonize.

My heart is truly blessed. I look out to the sanctuary and see my best
friend, Mark; and I look out and see Pastor James and his best childhood
friend, Chris. Two sets of best friends. We have all been through a great
deal, but God has brought us to this place where we can love one another,
love Him and be loved by Him.

The journey from Upper Room continued, and, like Christ's journey of rescue being commemorated, ours was one of both loneliness and
welcomed minimal community. As our local assembly's first Thirty-Six
Hours of Prayer vigil finished, these were my journal's concluding words:

April 23, 2011   *Holy Satuday 7:00 a.m.*

Glory be to the Father, and to the Son, and to the Holy Ghost. As it was
in the beginning, is now and ever shall be. World without end. Amen. Amen.

I had to blow the Communion candles out. They burned the entire thir-
ty-six hours.

For nearly a decade, our local assembly has held to both my teenage
vow and our communal commitment to keep the thirty-six-hour vigil.
Jesus was responsible for walking His steps from the Upper Room to the
emptied tomb, and each disciple, then and now, is responsible for walking His. It is not an issue of doing. It is an issue of being. It is not an issue
of God's approval or disapproval. It is an issue of allowing oneself to be
created by the Creator. We walk. God creates. We speak of the concepts
of this thing called Christianity, but it is the relationship of actuality that
God desires to have with the children of His breath. Before the Father,
at the place of advocacy, and filled and engulfed by Holy Spirit, it is the

relationship of actuality Brother desires to have with His mother, and brothers, and sisters. Do not allow any of these statements to alarm you, but instead allow them to sober you to a place of deeper knowledge of our Lord Who desires to fashion our spirits and glorify our flesh.

And so, only one thing remains: *an interlude of invitation to join my Upper Room to emptied-tomb journey of rescue.*

An Interlude of Invitation to Join My Journey

B efore an *RSVP* or *regret* is rendered, please acknowledge deep within every soul there is division from and longing for communion with the One larger than ourselves and with brothers and sisters in the struggle of life. Every division requires rescue, and the eternal estrangement of people from the God Who loves them necessitates the greatest of rescues. And so, whether we realize or not, each of us sets out on a journey to discover rescue. Thousands of years ago, the Messiah did the same. God descended into a journey, not to be rescued, but to offer rescue. The apostle Paul says the Messiah's journey to rescue each of us can be summed up in three words: *death, burial, and resurrection*. Whether the individual's journey to be rescued is active or passive, Jesus' journey of death, burial, and resurrection has brought rescue to all. You are now being invited to enter thirty-six hours from my personal journal. In the pages that follow, you will read my chronicling of Jesus' Upper Room to empty-tomb journey of rescue and my attempt, through vigil, to journey alongside creation's Rescuer. In the written testimony of my journey to be rescued and my stumbling over the messianic leaf of God's rescue that follows, perhaps you too will stumble, welcome rescue, and rise.

You are now cordially invited ...

My Upper Room to Empty-Tomb Journey to Rescue

Go and prepare the Passover

Thursday morning, April 13, 2017

And Jesus sent Peter and John, saying, "Go and prepare the Passover for us, so that we may eat it."

(LUKE 22:8 NASB)

I woke to find out one of my dear friends has died. He sang for the Lord here. Now he sings at His resurrected feet there. This morning and afternoon has been far different from any year before. Jesus asked Peter and John to go and make preparations for the Passover feast. Tonight we will receive the sacramental meal, then tomorrow and Saturday we allow God to create us as He will through the remembrance walk of our Messiah's death, burial, and anticipated resurrection.

I slept late today.

I satisfied this world's system without sin.

I ate. I drank.

I prepared for a neighbor's celebration.

I rested.

I read.

I napped.

Preparations have been made.

This year, I have allowed God to create me. In the past, I have tried, by doing, to earn God's approval. I have rested in fellowship. I have rested in holiness. I have surrendered, so God lets me be.

And so, this journey to resurrection culminates.

Death is not extinguishing the light
but merely putting out the lamp
because the dawn has come.

—Rabindranath Tagore

Taken, blessed, broken, and dispersed

Thursday evening, April 13, 2017

> *While they were eating, Jesus took some bread, and after a blessing,*
> *He broke it and gave it to the disciples, and said, "Take, eat; this is*
> *My body."*
> *And when He had taken a cup and given thanks, He gave it to*
> *them, saying, "Drink from it, all of you; for this is My blood of the*
> *covenant, which is poured out for many for forgiveness of sins.*
> *"But I say to you, I will not drink of this fruit of the vine from*
> *now on until that day when I drink it new with you in My Father's*
> *kingdom."*
>
> (MATTHEW 26:26–29 NASB)

A wise young man being created says, "We have no words to describe our God, so He is no more than simply, I Am." Most certainly, I Am is more than enough.

Father has taken Son, and Son has surrendered to Father's taking.

Father has taken Son and blessed Him.

Father has broken Son.

Father has dispersed Son as Gospel and as Holy Spirit.

It is now this taking, and blessing, and breaking, and dispersing God, Who whispers in the wind to us, saying, "Will you be taken? Will you be blessed? Will you be broken? Will you be dispersed?"

You are to be pretense no longer; you are to be revelatory.

Yet, unfortunately, it is God *we desire to take. To control.* It is the experience of God we long for. The experience becomes the god, rather than God, Himself. We cling to His tassels in our issues of blood. We bleed and bleed and bleed and bleed and overlook the blood of scourging, and crown, and dying that He journeyed through to rescue us, forever. Our bleeding lives within His blood, so we must not miss salvation while staring at the crowd and the occasion of the crucifixion. This is a reminder, but even in this reminder we can hear the accusation and chastisement from the one claiming to be a Creator, but who lives in the brokenness of creation. Accusation and chastisement does not bring divine creating to a not-yet-recreated, dying, lost soul.

Life comes from the One Who says, "My body has been taken, so take My body.

"My body has been blessed, so take My body.

"My body has been broken, so take My body.

"The dispersal of My body is among you, so now begin to be taken. Drink in the blessing. Drink in the brokenness. Allow the dispersal to be poured from the glory of Divine Revelation so very much alive in the existence of the truly living.

"Do not grab for Me. Allow Me to take you. My taking causes a looking away from the experience and finds Me within it. So look away, and be taken, and be blessed, and be broken, and be dispersed.

"The world will see Me, and hear Me, and know Me, and come to Me, too.

"Receive Eucharist and allow Eucharist to become within you. You are revelatory. You are the face of Christ."

To love as You love

People sit, and they stand, they kneel, and their hands are raised. This is holiness of God, and this is friendship with God. It is so hard to bridge the two. Either He is holy before us and we are overwhelmed and fall before Him. Or, God nestles in close to us, and we know of His friendship with us. Thankfully, grace teaches the heart to fear, yet immediately, lovingly relieves the heart of it by nestling each within omnipotence's beauty.

The Lord our God is Holy, so be Holy.

"No longer do I call you servants, but I call you friends."

There is to be a third in the same way that our God is Three.

There is a place for God's holiness, and we must welcome those Sinai moments. There is a place for God's friendship, and we must welcome those Upper Room moments. Still, there is a place for worship, a place where the dark cloud which holds God's feet lowers into the sanctuary. Instead of running in fear, we worship in friendship. God's holiness has made us well, has made us alive in Him. His death is familiar, but it is also holy. The only holy death there has ever been.

The empty.

The religious.

The filled to overflowing.

All who call Him Messiah have been each, and the Messiah has redeemed us.

My difficulty has never been in worship of God as friend, nor has it been in being overwhelmed by God's holiness. My difficulty is with my neighbors. I try, but I do not love them as He loves them ... and, yet, I so want to.

Lord, help me to love as You love. Perhaps my tears will help me to love them as You love them.

No longer dirty and captive

Awake, awake,
Clothe yourself in your strength, O Zion;
Clothe yourself in your beautiful garments,
O Jerusalem, the holy city;
For the uncircumcised and the unclean
Will no longer come into you.

Shake yourself from the dust, rise up,
O captive Jerusalem;
Loosen yourself from the chains around your neck,
O captive daughter of Zion.

For thus says the LORD, "You were sold for nothing and you
will be redeemed without money."

For thus says the LORD GOD, "My people went down at
the first into Egypt to reside there; then the Assyrian
oppressed them without cause."

"Now therefore, what do I have here," declares the LORD,
"seeing that My people have been taken away without
cause?"

Again the LORD declares, "Those who rule over them howl,
and My name is continually blasphemed all day long.

"Therefore, My people shall know My name; therefore in that
day I am the one who is speaking, 'Here I am.'"

How lovely on the mountains
Are the feet of him who brings good news,

Who announces peace
And brings good news of happiness,
Who announces salvation,
And says to Zion, "Your God reigns!"

Listen! Your watchmen lift up their voices,
They shout joyfully together;
For they will see with their own eyes
When the LORD restores Zion.

Break forth, shout joyfully together,
You waste places of Jerusalem;
For the LORD has comforted His people,
He has redeemed Jerusalem.

The LORD has bared His holy arm
In the sight of all the nations,
That all the ends of the earth may see
The salvation of our God.

Depart, depart, go out from there,
Touch nothing unclean;
Go out of the midst of her, purify yourselves,
You who carry the vessels of the LORD.

But you will not go out in haste,
Nor will you go as fugitives;
For the LORD will go before you,
And the God of Israel will be your rear guard.

Behold, My servant will prosper,
He will be high and lifted up and greatly exalted.

Just as many were astonished at you, My people,
So His appearance was marred more than any man
And His form more than the sons of men.

Thus He will sprinkle many nations,
Kings will shut their mouths on account of Him;
For what had not been told them they will see,
And what they had not heard they will understand.

Who has believed our message?
And to whom has the arm of the LORD been revealed?

For He grew up before Him like a tender shoot,
And like a root out of parched ground;
He has no stately form or majesty
That we should look upon Him,
Nor appearance that we should be attracted to Him.

He was despised and forsaken of men,
A man of sorrows and acquainted with grief;
And like one from whom men hide their face
He was despised, and we did not esteem Him.

Surely our griefs He Himself bore,
And our sorrows He carried;
Yet we ourselves esteemed Him stricken,
Smitten of God, and afflicted.

But He was pierced through for our transgressions,
He was crushed for our iniquities;
The chastening for our well-being fell upon Him,
And by His scourging we are healed.

All of us like sheep have gone astray,
Each of us has turned to His own way;
But the LORD has caused the iniquity of us all
To fall on Him.

He was oppressed and He was afflicted,
Yet He did not open His mouth;
Like a lamb that is led to slaughter,
And like a sheep that is silent before its shearers,
So He did not open His mouth.

By oppression and judgment He was taken away;
And as for His generation, who considered
That He was cut off out of the land of the living
For the transgression of my people, to whom the stroke
was due?

His grave was assigned with wicked men,
Yet He was with a rich man in His death,
Because He had done no violence,
Nor was there any deceit in His mouth.

But the LORD was pleased
To crush Him, putting Him to grief;
If He would render Himself as a guilt offering,
He will see His offspring,
He will prolong His days,
And the good pleasure of the LORD will prosper in His hand.

As a result of the anguish of His soul,
He will see it and be satisfied;
By His knowledge the Righteous One,
My Servant, will justify the many,
As He will bear their iniquities.

Therefore, I will allot Him a portion with the great,
And He will divide the booty with the strong;
Because He poured out Himself to death,
And was numbered with the transgressors;
Yet He Himself bore the sin of many,
And interceded for the transgressors.

(ISAIAH 52 & 53 NASB)

What will it be like when the call goes up to receive the fullness of the holiness of God and the glorification of creation's bodies? Will we all be in Jerusalem? What will it be like when sin is gone, when pursuit of foolishness no longer exists? What will the feeling feel like when the press is no longer on our shoulders and chests and the swirling of our minds has ceased? To clothe ourselves in garments of beauty, clothes that will for the first time truly fit.

To be dusty no more.

To be captive no more.

Will the necklace around our necks be crosses any longer, or will we even remember the cross and its weight? We have looked to it. We have shouldered it. Will Jesus say to us, "It is time to loosen yourself from that chain around your neck, O captive daughter of Zion"? Is the cross the chain we carry? Will we need its reminder any longer? Are we to carry it here, and then will He call for us to put it away forever there?

I do not know. So, I will continue to carry it until the Messiah cries, "Awake, awake!"

What is the nothing for which humanity was sold? Rebellion is nothing. Saying what God did not say is nothing. Questioning what is certain is nothing. Lust for flesh is nothing. Lust flowing from the eye is nothing. Pride is nothing. Taking what is not to be taken is nothing. Eating what is not to be eaten is nothing. Giving nothing to the innocent and completing the cycle of sin and death is nothing.

Humanity was sold for nothing.

Nothing should never be allowed to characterize the existence of the living.

No commerce established by humanity was ever, nor ever will be, able to rescue humanity. Commerce sees no need for rescue or redemption. Rescue affords redemption through perfect death, burial, and resurrection. There has been only one. What begins in settling's flow results in oppression; and oppression of even those who have innocently entered into a land not their own are in need of redemption.

We have nothing *here*, and yet we are *here* ... and as exiles *here*, He desires to have us.

Then, *here,* as it is *there*, can become pure again through fire; and then we can be both *here* and *there* with Him.

Here mutates His name. *Here* makes fun. *Here* ignores. *Here* turns from Him and turns those from Him.

And so, I AM says, "*Here* I am."

And God's children climb to the highest so that the song of God can be sung and descend over all. Our feet are shod with the gospel of peace, and happiness, and salvation. Our laces sing, "Our God reigns!" To those who will hear, we call them to untie the laces.

Son will stand with mother.

Husband will stand with wife.

Neighbor will stand with neighbor.

And they who hear will all raise their hands together—in freedom, with laces untied.

There is a call upon the world to listen. Those who watch the East for the coming Messiah, Who has already come, have lifted their voices as they have for years. Lifting now, as they were lifted then, their voices in martyrdom rise as God's perfect witnesses. As once lifted, they lift their voices in peace. Not even calm is permitted to silence them.

There is a man from so far away who was changed here. God has called him home.

There is a woman who was stolen from; she is violated no longer. God has called her home.

The Watchmen's voices lift, as once lifted.

When Christ shall come with shout of acclamation what joy shall fill my heart.

Then I shall bow in humble adoration and there proclaim, "My God how great Thou art!"

Those who are His pursue this world's kingdom and kingdoms no longer. Why should we? We have no part with them. The road to the rule and reign of God is paved with uncomeliness. There is nothing to draw us to salvation's road. It is a road of rejection. It is a road of stripes. Still, it is the only road that both heals and leads to healing. Somehow that healing, though, is not all we need. The world would say, "Yes, be healed. Be healed and receive your healing and its fullness." But there is no fullness to physical healing. It will eventually result in decay, and decay will eventually result in death. Even now, what was once stifled begins to call out again, "Surrender to weight's push and not to the faith you have claimed." It says, "You are a liar, and you are dying."

I am dying, and so I am in need of healing. Healing soothes the soul and calls to new creation. When the flares of agony have begun to smolder and the open sores of tribulation have become bruises, the healed are neither snuffed out nor are they broken off. Those that walk healing's road and are healed walk even further with our Messiah, Who, in so many ways, has become our Cyrene, and we find ourselves in healing's greatest revelation: *new creation via Abba's breath.*

We stand with the One Who poured out Himself to death, Whose dead Person numbered Him among the transgressors; yet, He, as He took on the sin of many, brought rescue to the transgressors. He, and they, and we are transgressors to the kings and kingdoms of this world, but to the King and His place and position of rule and reign, we are princes and priests. To the Bearer, the Intercessor, we are brothers; we are sisters. We are sons and daughters of the Living God.

His Kingdom is ours, and ours is His Kingdom ...

On earth as it is in heaven.

Glory to the Lamb Who was slain, our rescuing, resurrected King.

If I don't wash you ...

Now before the Feast of the Passover, Jesus knowing that His hour had come that He would depart out of this world to the Father, having loved His own who were in the world, He loved them to the end.

During supper, the devil, having already put into the heart of Judas Iscariot, the son of Simon, to betray Him, Jesus, knowing that the Father had given all things into His hands, and that He had come forth from God and was going back to God, got up from supper, and laid aside His garments; and taking a towel, He girded Himself.

Then He poured water into the basin, and began to wash the disciples' feet and to wipe them with the towel with which He was girded.

So He came to Simon Peter. He said to Him, "Lord, do You wash my feet?"

Jesus answered and said to him, "What I do you do not realize now, but you will understand hereafter."

Peter said to Him, "Never shall You wash my feet!" Jesus answered him, "If I do not wash you, you have no part with Me."

Simon Peter said to Him, "Lord, then wash not only my feet, but also my hands and my head."

Jesus said to him, "He who has bathed needs only to wash his feet, but is completely clean; and you are clean, but not all of you." For He knew the one who was betraying Him; for this reason, He said, "Not all of you are clean."

So when He had washed their feet, and taken His garments and reclined at the table again, He said to them, "Do you know what I have done to you? You call Me Teacher and Lord; and you are right, for so I am. If I then, the Lord and the Teacher, washed your feet, you also ought to wash one another's feet. For I gave you an example that you also should do as I did to you. Truly, truly, I say to you, a slave is not greater than his master, nor is one who is sent greater than the one who sent him. If you know these things, you are blessed if you do them."

(JOHN 13:1–17 NASB)

The wind howls. It has been howling for hours. I have no idea what is happening outside, but I believe and I know that Holy Spirit is moving with a greatness around, over and through this place, but more importantly among this people. Those who are here throughout these hours, now and then, in and out, here and not here, always present, will know the winds of the Divine.

To wash and be washed.

A new teacher, a new mentor, a new Paul recently said to a room full of bondservants that we are not servants of the Lord but servants of one another. He served us in His death, in His burial, in His resurrection, in His ascension, in His advocacy, in His waiting, in His one day return. If He has served us, then we should also serve one another. In the context of this Scripture, whether I am or am not a servant of the *Lord* is not the issue. The lesson is to be a servant of *humanity*. Those we love, we are to serve ... and love deepens. Those we do not love, we are to serve ... and then love is conceived, gestated, and born. Those who are *more than*, we are to serve ... and they become *as much as*. Those who are *less than*, we are to serve ... and they become *as much as*. Those who are well known, we serve ... and they will be known as they are known. Those we do not know, we serve ... and they become the dearest. The close and the outcast, the rich and the poor, the young and the old, all are to be served. They are not to be grouped. They are to be loved.

And in loving, we are serving.

And in serving, we are loving.

And the circular rhythm of the Divine Servant declares life more abundant.

Humble us, O God, in our arrogance. Show us with the tools of nakedness and water, rather than calamity and pain, that we are to serve one another with Your love.

We too often only see the Messiah high and lifted up, when the Messiah is also naked and washing before us. Before there can be ascent into God's glory, we must descend into God's greatness. Then there is no longer a desire to ascend. Stripped down is adornment. Adornment in the beginning results in destruction, thievery, and murder. Descent into cleansing and servitude results in communion over the miraculous because communion with God's glory is the only miraculous necessary ... *it is more than enough.*

His enough is more.

So more than enough is a perfection that is to be found in the place of naked hand upon naked foot bathed in the purity of naked, holy waters.

In communion, the Messiah's siblings sing:

I am Thine, O Lord, I have heard Thy voice,
And it told Thy love to me;
But I long to rise in the arms of faith
And be closer drawn to Thee.

Draw me nearer, nearer blessed Lord,
To the cross where Thou hast died;
Draw me nearer, nearer, nearer blessed Lord,
To Thy precious, bleeding side.

Consecrate me now to Thy service, Lord,
By the pow'r of grace divine;
Let my soul look up with a steadfast hope,
And my will be lost in Thine.

Oh, the pure delight of a single hour
That before Thy throne I spend,
When I kneel in prayer, and with Thee, my God
I commune as friend with friend!

There are depths of love that I cannot know
Till I cross the narrow sea;

There are heights of joy that I may not reach
Till I rest in peace with Thee.
(Draw Me Nearer, *Fanny Crosby, 1875; public domain*)

The rising into the arms of faith that we would be closer drawn to Christ is not from a place of higher and higher but from the ground as we hold foul feet. To serve, rather than be served, and to give one's life as a ransom for many. This is where we are closer drawn to Christ. Only where there is service to others is there the elimination of the talk that cries, "Which one of us is the greatest?" The greatest is the one who discerns Holy Spirit's voice and then speaks revelation over the called. The greatest is the one who is able to serve the meal, while never leaving the Teacher's feet. The greatest is the one who never has to move farther back but tends the door and makes the way for the greatest among us. The greatest doesn't know the widow; she is the widow. The greatest doesn't adopt the orphan but is the orphan. The greatest does not release the prisoner but is shackled with him, and as the walls fall at the sound of praise, the greatest and his companion stay in the center of the jail because no jail, nor jailer, has ever been able to imprison them.

Our feet have been washed.

We do likewise.

Sing to us Lord that we would sing Your song

Jesus spoke these things, and lifting up His eyes to heaven, He said, "Father, the hour has come; glorify Your Son, that the Son may glorify You, even as You gave Him authority over all flesh, that to all whom You have given Him, He may give eternal life. This is eternal life, that they may know You, the only true God, and Jesus Christ whom You have sent. I glorified You on the earth, having accomplished the work which You have given Me to do. Now, Father, glorify Me together with Yourself, with the glory which I had with You before the world was.

"I have manifested Your name to the men whom You gave Me out of the world; they were Yours and You gave them to Me, and they have kept Your word. Now they have come to know that everything You have given Me is from You; for the words which You gave Me I have given to them; and they received them and truly understood that I came forth from You, and they believed that You sent Me. I ask on their behalf; I do not ask on behalf of the world, but of those whom You have given Me; for they are Yours; and all things that are Mine are Yours, and Yours are Mine; and I have been glorified in them. I am no longer in the world; and yet they themselves are in the world, and I come to You. Holy Father, keep them in Your name, the name which You have given Me, that they may be one even as We are. While I was with them, I was keeping them in Your name which You have given Me; and I guarded them and not one of them perished but the son of perdition, so that the Scripture would be fulfilled. But now I come to You; and these things I speak in the world so that they may have My joy made full in themselves. I have given them Your word; and the world has hated them, because they are not of the world, even as I am not of the world. I do not ask You to take them out of the world, but to keep them from the evil one. They are not of the world, even as I am not of the world. Sanctify them in the truth; Your word is truth. As

You sent Me into the world, I also have sent them into the world. For their sakes I sanctify Myself, that they themselves also may be sanctified in truth.

"I do not ask on behalf of these alone, but for those also who believe in Me through their word; that they may all be one; even as You, Father, are in Me and I in You, that they also may be in Us, so that the world may believe that You sent Me. The glory which You have given Me I have given to them, that they may be one, just as We are one; I in them and You in Me, that they may be perfected in unity, so that the world may know that You sent Me, and loved them, even as You have loved Me. Father, I desire that they also, whom You have given Me, be with Me where I am, so that they may see My glory which You have given Me, for You loved Me before the foundation of the world.

"O righteous Father, although the world has not known You, yet I have known You; and these have known that You sent Me; and I have made Your name known to them, and will make it known, so that the love with which You loved Me may be in them, and I in them."

(JOHN 17 NASB)

Vulnerability ceases to exist where there is community because community will not hurt, or cut, or strike, or belittle. Community only loves. Love is community's offering.

For thousands of years, the hour to come was looked to and spoken of. Now the hour has come. Glorification has dawned.

Glory is obscured by the darkest of clouds.

The cloudiness is not covert. It is ominous. It is coming. Wave upon wave, it is a thickening. The thickening of the enemy's approach is not designed to kill but to call to quit. To sin. Then all will be creation's, until creation destroys itself and all life will die. They are obscured by their own clouds.

The hour has come.

Glory will reign, but it must proceed first.

Prayer's immaturity is seen, amidst existence's circumstantial vacuum, as a response of swirling trepidation. The maturity of prayer is characterized by one who speaks the divine tool in motion, in order to prepare before entering the vortex. Our Messiah is mature.

He prays for community within His vulnerability.

Within the flesh, the Creator holds authority over all flesh, both humanity's and His own. He is the only One Whose Spirit-willingness always trumped flesh-weakness. Still, He had to battle. Flesh was not yet glorified. But with the glorification of the resurrected Messiah comes realization of eternal life.

Life is not pursued. It is not climbed. It is not sounded or descended into. It is not reached by the greatest of speeds or the highest of leaps. It does not waste away nor can it be preserved, for Life is already preservation without need to be preserved. Life cannot be bought nor contained, but it can be offered and housed. Life alone is eternal. Death had a beginning, as did existence. Creation begins. Creation exists. Creation dies. Creation continues. The Creator always was, always is, always will be. Eternal life has and is given.

Eternal life is knowing the One Who created and continues to create to the point of glorification. Eternal life is knowing Jesus Messiah.

From conception, to gestation, to birth, to growth, to submission, to maturity, to manhood, to baptism, to transition, to kingdom at hand, to miracles, to ministry, to Jerusalem, to the Upper Room, to Gethsemane, to the Sanhedrin, to Pilate, to Herod, to scourging, to Pilate, to the long walk, to Golgotha, to the cross, to Psalm 22, to "Son, behold your mother; mother, behold your son," to "It is accomplished," to giving up His Spirit, to lying still, to claiming the keys, to cracking open death's seal with life, Jesus Messiah has glorified the Father on the earth, having accomplished the work which Father gave Son to do.

And thus our Messiah is glorified.

The whistle sounds His arrival, His accomplishment, and His arrival once more.

The Two are One in glory and eternity, and we have seen it so manifested before us for centuries.

We hold His name. They held it then. We hold it now. We hold it together. They were given to Son by Father. We are given to Son by Father. They kept Word. We keep Word. We are community together, and all we have is from Him.

Everything.

Is there true understanding? Yes, for the understanding we possess had its nature generated in God. Word is not to be held, or handled, or controlled. Word is to be believed. Belief frees Word to provide, to heal, to manifest, to welcome, to surrender, to cleanse, to bring life. It must be so, or He will not be able to heal here just as He was unable to heal there. The flat of the Mount must be our desire. It was there that His power was coming from Him and healing them all.

Our community is not the empire's, and the empire's community is not ours. They do not desire ours, though they attempt to impose. Yet, their imposition has no effect because while they attempt to grasp for what is ours, we have no desire for what is theirs. The Creator is Lord of all creation.

And now I stop.

I have read this prayer, this High Priestly prayer, time and again. So many years ago, Jesus sang it over me and over each of us. Yet, I must keep looking over, over my arm to the red words on the page beside me to offer commentary for words I do not know. The Messiah has sung these words over me, and still, I do not know the lyrics of the song He wrote and sang for them, and He wrote and sang for me. I will know them, and I will allow the Lyricist to write them on my heart as He sings *me* as His living poem.

I know they are words of unity, and I know they are words of intercession. I know they are words for the disciples then and for the disciples now. I know they are words that speak of the glory of the Father and the glory of the Son. Still, I long to know the words, word for word, that have been sung over me, that have been sung over them.

In His agony, He sang for me.

In His agony, He sang for them.

We must learn the notes with love. Like a proud parent of an aspiring musician, upon our missed notes, is the Messiah's grace. Along with the Messiah, we will sing creation's song as the hymn becomes our heart.

O righteous Father, although
The world has not known You, yet
I have known You; and these
Have known that You sent Me.

And I have made Your name
Known to them, and will make it
Known, so that the love with
Which You loved Me may be in
Them, and I in them.

(John 17:25; 26 NASB)

Gethsemane

Then Jesus came with them to a place called Gethsemane, and said to His disciples, "Sit here while I go over there and pray." And He took with Him Peter and the two sons of Zebedee, and began to be grieved and distressed. Then He said to them, "My soul is deeply grieved, to the point of death; remain here and keep watch with Me."

And He went a little beyond them, and fell on His face and prayed, saying, "My Father, if it is possible, let this cup pass from Me; yet not as I will, but as You will." And He came to the disciples and found them sleeping, and said to Peter, "So, you men could not keep watch with Me for one hour? Keep watching and praying that you may not enter into temptation; the spirit is willing, but the flesh is weak."

He went away again a second time and prayed, saying, "My Father, if this cannot pass away unless I drink it, Your will be done." Again He came and found them sleeping, for their eyes were heavy. And He left them again, and went away and prayed a third time, saying the same thing once more. Then He came to the disciples and said to them, "Are you still sleeping and resting? Behold, the hour is at hand and the Son of Man is being betrayed into the hands of sinners. Get up, let us be going; behold, the one who betrays Me is at hand!"

While He was still speaking, behold, Judas, one of the twelve, came up accompanied by a large crowd with swords and clubs, who came from the chief priests and elders of the people. Now he who was betraying Him gave them a sign, saying, "Whomever I kiss, He is the one; seize Him." Immediately, Judas went to Jesus and said, "Hail, Rabbi!" and kissed Him. And Jesus said to him, "Friend, do what you have come for." Then they came and laid hands on Jesus and seized Him.

And behold, one of those who were with Jesus reached and drew out his sword, and struck the slave of the high priest and cut off his ear. Then Jesus said to him, "Put your sword back into its place; for all those who take up the sword shall perish by the sword. Or do you think that I cannot appeal to My Father, and He will at once put at

My disposal more than twelve legions of angels? How then will the
Scriptures be fulfilled, which say that it must happen this way?"

At that time Jesus said to the crowds, "Have you come out with
swords and clubs to arrest Me as you would against a robber? Every
day I used to sit in the temple teaching and you did not seize Me.
But all this has taken place to fulfill the Scriptures of the prophets."
Then all the disciples left Him and fled.

(MATTHEW 26:36–56 NASB)

Gethsemane is the purification of Eden. In Gethsemane, the head of
the serpent spoken of in Eden is crushed. Golgotha was not the place
of the crushing. It was Gethsemane. It was in Gethsemane that Christ
settled into His resolution. In Gethsemane, the Messiah became resolute.
Satan would try to judge Him into submission. Jesus signed His own war-
rant. Satan would try to beat Him into submission. Jesus pushed Himself
up on the whipping post. Satan tried to mock Jesus into submission. Jesus
received the world's crown and robe. Satan tried to exhaust Christ into
submission. He carried His cross with God and neighbor. Satan tried to
submit the Christ through pain. He received the nails. Satan tried to call
the Christ from His cross with the pride of life. Jesus did not leap from
Temple peak or cross's beams. Satan tried to bring Christ to complete
Psalm 22 with the words, "My God, my God, why have You forsaken
Me?" Jesus let the Psalm play to its completion and said with dignity and
victory, "It is accomplished."

Gethsemane was the place of the Messiah's resolution.

Though it stands as a certainly arduous journey, Golgotha simply
revealed the cup that had been welcomed.

There is always a cup *that keeps us from* and a cup *that brings us to*.
The reception of strength to endure always finds its humanity in the less-
than-desired drink that fills the *brings us to* vessel. Weakness stands as the
primary fluid to strip away the ambiguity of excuse and resistance.

From the less-than-desired, He drank deeply, and the Messiah was
brought to.

An attempt to watch and pray lest I fall into temptation: The love with which God looks upon me

"Then He said to them, 'My soul is deeply grieved, to the point of death; remain here and keep watch with Me.'"

(MATTHEW 26:38 NASB)

Your love is something that has always been there God, but it is also something very new to me. I have always known that You love me, but the way I have received Your love has been through seeing You as an approving or disapproving God. If I did well, You approved, and Your love was released upon me. If I did not do well, You disapproved, and while Your love was still there, I shut myself from it. I believed it was kept from me, because I had failed. I have been so very wrong.

You love me.

You just love me.

Good deeds and bad deeds.

You say to me, "Stop. Stop, and simply receive My love. My love is not an exercise. It just surrounds you. It is silence. It is joy. It is Godly sorrow. It is hope. It is the inspiration from your mind to your fingers. I'm writing for you. Son, I love you. Simply receive My love, and stop trying to fill the time.

"I love you."

And I love you too, Lord.

An attempt to watch and pray lest I fall into temptation: The gifts God's love has given

You have given me the gift of good rest.

You gave me a Paul, to me, a Timothy.

You have given me the gift of news that is good and bad. I rejoice that Jake sings before Your feet, but I wish he were still able to sing for You in this room. You have given me peace in the morning and throughout this day at Jake's passing, and You have given me tears of compassion this evening. You gave me the testimony of people who listened to Jake's praise for You throughout this day. You gave me compassion from folks for me, because they knew and know I loved and love him.

You gave me food and drink.

You gave me provision. I'm valued far more than the birds and the lilies, and I see how well You care for them.

In this moment, a friend tells me You gave him a song. Thank you, Lord, for giving.

You gave me flesh of my flesh and bone of my bone.

You gave me sons to love, who also love You.

You gave me words from a compassionate man, a man who, each time I read his words, is used by You to create a more compassionate me.

You gave me rest, and a bed, and a home, and covering.

You gave me sleep.

You gave me community.

You gave me Eucharist.

You gave me a flock that is Yours, and You entrusted them to me. I will be a good shepherd.

You gave me this evening.

You gave me kisses, and You gave me hugs.

You gave me this silence.

And I thank You, my Lord and my God, my Messiah, my Savior, my All.

An attempt to watch and pray lest I fall into temptation: A work of grace, fruitful beyond my human capacity alone

Over the years, I have tried to build my own table and place my own chairs. I have tried to set my own place and prepare my own meal. I have set the meal before myself and declared it good. I ate and told myself I was satisfied. Then, and only after all that, did I look to You and seek Your approval.

God, it is Your wisdom, and Your strength, and Your grace through which, and by which, I have life, and breath, and being—by and through You alone, God. I lean into You.

You are my all in all.

You are my breath.

You are my being.

You are my movement.

You are my thoughts.

You are my call.

You are my strength.

You are my peace.

You are my rest.

You are the wind that howls behind me, and the dunamis that goes before me.

You are God, Who keeps me.

You are the One Who tells me who I am. I no longer define myself. Tell me who I am. Tell me what to say, or nothing at all. Tell me when to say it, or not at all. Lead me. Stand still before me. I am yours, for You have made Yourself mine.

Your grace alone, God.

Glory be to Your Holy Name.

An attempt to watch and pray lest I fall into temptation: An inventory of thought and choice

My first thoughts as I woke this morning, God, were thoughts of guilt. I saw that my Paul has called me two times prior to waking and I immediately thought, "He will be disappointed. I did not rise early to worship Thee." It is improper to feel that way, when You, God, have given me sweet rest. Please forgive my desire to do, rather than be, while in the sweet rest You so graciously provided.

When the news of Jake's passing came, I was disappointed, but I held peace just as peace was holding me. The news was bad. The news was good. I continue to cling to these words:

> *Death is not extinguishing the light*
> *but merely putting out the lamp*
> *because the dawn has come.*

—Rabindranath Tagore

I have thought about this for days now, and in this review of this day, I believe it is more than fine to rest here.

What is my fear and obsession with death? It used to be some idea of heroic going, but You put that to rest. It may be the idea of pain, or not being able to breathe, or being alone when it occurs, but if strength is made perfect in weakness, and You are my breath, and You will never leave nor forsake me, and You have given so many by my side, then what is my fear? Is it the vulnerability in which I will find myself when I reach the point of death? That is ridiculous.

God, You have stirred my heart to the peaceful moment where sons will be blessed, legs will be drawn deeply in, last breaths will be exhaled, and a gathering unto my people will occur. I do not know if this is your promise to me, but it is my surrendered and faithful hope in You.

Glory to You, my God and King.

An attempt to watch and pray lest I fall into temptation: The healing touch of the forgiving God, Who removes my heart's burdens

How powerful this prayer is.

That is not a question. It is reality.

The greatest removal of burdens is in not having to have an answer to everything. When only questions stand, questions are swept away with the present comfort of You, my God. You have forgiven me. You forgave me long ago. So long ago that my forgiveness was spoken while You were dying to rescue me. So long ago that my forgiveness existed in Eden's sacrifice. So long ago that my forgiveness was present as You set sun, moon, and stars in the sky for signs and seasons. These same signs and seasons that have always pointed me to Your invisible attributes, Lord.

Your healing touch ... it is most certainly upon me.

I can feel Your peace rushing through me these most recent days. It was always there, but I had to be made to lie down in the green pastures, and be led by Your right hand beside the quiet waters. I had to come to know that neither the valley's deathly shadows nor the glory of the highest mountain peaks control my life. You control my life. And, just as You are greater than the Temple, there is also One Who is greater than heights and shadows. You are the Greater Than.

I don't have to ask, Lord. I just have to surrender.

I surrender.

These moments of Thirty-Six Hours of Prayer vigil used to be weight—and I am certain weight will come throughout these seconds, and minutes, and hours, and days, and darkness and light—but for now, God, it is not weight. What I know is comfort and peace. In the midst of death and dying, I already am knowing resurrection.

Hallelujah to the Risen Lord.

An attempt to watch and pray lest I fall into temptation: The following day and God's loving desire for my life

What will the following day hold? Typically, the covers are pulled tightly to my chin by this time, but tonight will be tomorrow very soon. As today becomes tomorrow, there will be no tomorrow because there is no sleep, there is no turning away from Your passion. With your passion, today is comprised of thirty-six hours. There may be periods of weakened flesh, other times of willing spirits, and still other times of divine rest, but until Sunday's resurrection comes, there will be no following day.

So, Lord, how do I live this next extended day in accord with Your loving desire? I simply spend it with You. I can hear what seems to be howling winds outside this temple of sorts. Hours from now, a world that does not know You, or that has made the choice to suppress Your name, will awake. Their sounds will growl, gurgle, and roar. Yet, I prefer the complimentary sounds of the bird and the cricket. Your desire for my life is to spend every moment with You.

Some of the moments will be spent with you alone.

Some moments I will share Your love—which is Your Person—with others.

Some of the moments we will do both.

Your desire, God, I long to live.

You are God alone.

An attempt to watch and pray lest I fall into temptation: Far more with me, than I with Him

How does one conclude time with the God Who never concludes—the God Who is the same yesterday, today, and forever? You are eternal, O God, and so is my surrender to Your Lordship. The child believes the "amen" to be "goodbye." Such is not so.

So eternally with You, I do not conclude. I simply say ...

Let it be so.

Then the kingdom of humanity showed itself as it always does: *out of control*. It spun and swirled, waved swords and cut off ears. The kingdom of the Messiah held still and healed. It did, and it does. Then and now, the Messiah's kingdom teaches and calls its citizens to beat their swords into plowshares; and to run if they must, but always know they can repent and return.

Why was this night different from any other night?

It was not.

Jesus was still Messiah, still teacher. He did so in the fields, and He did so in the Temple courts, and He did so in Gethsemane, and He would do so on the cross. Nothing was different from any other night.

The mouth that received the wine-drenched piece of bread from Jesus' hand is the same mouth that rested on Jesus' cheek. Nothing was different. It is a kiss that confirms that Jesus is Messiah and a kiss that confirms humanity's betrayal of the Messiah.

He extends His hands and exerts the greatest power of humanity and heaven. To surrender to ones who hold no power over you ... such is the greatest strength.

We walk into the darkness.

Darkness I

Friday, April 14, 2017, Midnight

If I say, "Surely the darkness will overwhelm me,
And the light around me will be night,"
Even the darkness is not dark to You,
And the night is as bright as the day.
Darkness and light are alike to You.
For You formed my inward parts;
You wove me in my mother's womb.
I will give thanks to You, for I am fearfully and wonderfully made;
Wonderful are Your works,
And my soul knows it very well.

(PSALM 139:11–14 NASB)

Like that night, a handful remain. Most have scattered, but none is better than the other. There is but one Messiah. All are scattered, sinful sheep in need of Ezekiel's Shepherd. Just like those before us, we find ourselves running from the darkness of Gethsemane to the deeper darkness of a new day's crucifixion.

Though there was darkness, His death was during the day.

O, that we would make it to morning.

How many times have I allowed myself to be overwhelmed by crucifixion's darkness rather than be bathed by the light of the night? Two lights are in the sky, not one. The moon is just as majestically qualified to reign over the sky as the sun. Still, each is only creation, and it is the Creator's presence alone that calls us to wholeness and the settledness of peace.

Before confrontation, when the darkness of evil surrounded us, we surrendered and slept.

Now, in the midst of confrontation and anxiety, darkness's goodness cannot coax us to sleep.

So often, when the spirit is willing, flesh reveals its weakness. When flesh is willing, spirit hides and looks out for any who seeks to find him. It is in the hiding that we hear the Creator of the sun and the moon, light and darkness, approaching us. We are terrified, but neither light nor darkness affects the cool of the day for Him. The inward parts God formed are no more hidden behind this pretense of claimed holiness than they were while in mother's womb being woven by the Creator's hand.

The distaff and spindle fit God's palms nicely, just as nicely as our need for sacrifice.

If we can look away from darkness, look away from light, if we can just fix our gaze on both our nakedness and the sacrificial covering the Messiah has made ready for us, then our hearts will submissively cry in accord with the nature of the One, "Even the darkness is not dark to You. Day is dark, and night is light. You will not be pawed at by either. They are the same to You." The One who saves is the same One Who created and creates, and so we give thanks.

The fear of my wonderful making is not in the enveloping darkness nor is it in the scorching light. My wonderful making is in the Maker. I am driven to the ground in fear at the sight of His feet, but with His right hand He lifts me and assures me, "Do not be afraid."

I am not afraid of the dark.

I believe.

I am not afraid of the dark.

Help my unbelief.

Darkness II

Now when the sun was going down, a deep sleep fell upon Abram; and behold, terror and great darkness fell upon him. God said to Abram, "Know for certain that your descendants will be strangers in a land that is not theirs, where they will be enslaved and oppressed four hundred years. But I will also judge the nation whom they will serve, and afterward they will come out with many possessions. As for you, you shall go to your fathers in peace; you will be buried at a good old age. Then in the fourth generation they will return here, for the iniquity of the Amorite is not yet complete."

It came about when the sun had set, that it was very dark, and behold, there appeared a smoking oven and a flaming torch which passed between these pieces. On that day, the LORD made a covenant with Abram, saying,

"To your descendants I have given this land,

From the river of Egypt as far as the great river, the river Euphrates:

the Kenite and the Kenizzite and the Kadmonite

and the Hittite and the Perizzite and the Rephaim

and the Amorite and the Canaanite and the Girgashite and the Jebusite."

(GENESIS 15:12–21 NASB)

God, my brother prays for Your protection to be upon us, but how can You be protection for us when You fall upon us as terror and great darkness? How can You be some kind of defense when Your coming is ushered in by a darkness that is the deepest? How so, Lord? I do not doubt. I simply seek the answer or comfort.

Does terror and great darkness always accompany sleep? It certainly does for some. Such is the reason so many dread the night and cannot sleep through it. They would rather be awake and face what they dread

to face than sleep within it and be subject to it. Awake and hiding is pre-
ferred to asleep and without the ability to strike the kind of blow they will
never have the courage to strike. Somehow they believe the sight of ter-
rible darkness is a more controllable state than, through sleep, detaching
themselves from it. Both are the enemy's lies.

If honest, I would admit I am among them.

But I, too, must overcome.

Staying awake and hiding no more faces the darkness than the
attempt to overcome it through slumbering avoidance. In addition, the
terror and great darkness that accompanies God's beautiful covenant is
something we should neither hide from nor close our eyes to. Somehow,
if we are to experience the protection God's darkness provides, we must
learn to embrace it.

*Lord, You give Your children sweet rest. Peaceful sleep is truly a gift from
You. So, before Abram ever experiences the terror of great darkness, You settle
him into a deep sleep. Who were those You spoke to in dreams and visions?
Certainly, Abram was one. Was not Joseph and Daniel both those who could
discern the Divine voice within dreams? They held no fears as Pharaoh and
Nebuchadnezzar did. Did not Ezekiel have dreams, and Joseph, and Peter,
and Ananias, and Paul, and the Revelator while on the Island of Patmos?
All had beautiful dreams, and all were told not to be afraid of the terror of
the great darkness that preceded You. Certainly, not all darkness is evil. Only
when darkness is welcomed will the smoking oven and the flaming torch be
permitted to pass through the bleeding pieces of our lives.*

*When it is You, Lord, we can and must welcome the fear. We must
welcome the terror of Your presence. We must welcome the great darkness
that surrounds You. We have grown so familiar with the occasional wisps
of Your glory that pass us by that we have minimized them and taken them
for granted. Some would say, "This cannot be so." They are correct because
even a wisp of Your glory would cause our cleft-hidden faces to shine so
brightly that others would have to turn away or cry for us to veil ourselves.
Through mutual admiration, we have fooled one another. By saying, "The*

Lord is among us," and not engaging with the One Who actually is, we have commercialized, and institutionalized, and cauterized Your presence which You desire to freely move among us. We claim a form that masquerades the light of Your presence while Your presence is not actually manifest; and we are either too afraid or too ignorant to welcome the darkness that declares Your greatest revelations.

Before creation came into being, Your Spirit hovered in darkness over the face of the formless and void waters of pre-creation.

Before the blood covenant with Abram, darkness descended upon him.

In Your post-Exodus coming down upon Sinai, clouds of darkness covered Horeb's pinnacle.

At the dedication of Solomon's Temple, so much darkness was present that the priests could not enter its newly constructed courts.

Gethsemane was bathed in darkness.

Jerusalem was palled in darkness from noon until 3:00 p.m.

Before dawn, the women returned to the tomb in darkness.

From the Messiah's bruised and darkened side, blood and water flowed, and into darkness flowed rescuing resurrection. It did so to bring us not from darkness and into light, but so we could grow content within either, because neither dictates who we are. Sometimes You do come in light—a light so blinding we are struck from our horses of arrogance and murderous acts. Sometimes You do come in darkness, and we must be encouraged to not fear. Be it darkness or light, within either, our focus should always be Your presence and Your revelation. It is not light that blinds or darkness that makes us afraid. You cause the seeing to become blind and the blind to become seeing. You cause the proud to become fearful and the fearful to become bold.

And so, we return to our original questions: How can You be protection for us when You are falling upon us as terror and great darkness? How can You be some kind of defense when Your coming is ushered in by the deepest of darkness? How so, Lord? Your light and your darkness are simply precursors of your presence and revelation. We stand firm knowing that Your darkness brings sweet sleep and bowed knees, and Your light brings bowed *knees and a restoration that calls for the elimination of fear. We hold. We wait within both. You have not left us comfortless. Light and darkness are trumpet blasts. After, we stand firm and wait for Your presence and Your revelation.*

Glory to You, God, over the darkness and the light.

Darkness III

"See, I have taught you statutes and judgments just as the LORD my God commanded me, that you should do thus in the land where you are entering to possess it. So keep and do them, for that is your wisdom and your understanding in the sight of the peoples who will hear all these statutes and say, 'Surely, this great nation is a wise and understanding people.' For what great nation is there that has a god so near to it as is the LORD our God whenever we call on Him? Or what great nation is there that has statutes and judgments as righteous as this whole law which I am setting before you today?

"Only give heed to yourself and keep your soul diligently, so that you do not forget the things which your eyes have seen and they do not depart from your heart all the days of your life; but make them known to your sons and your grandsons. Remember the day you stood before the LORD your God at Horeb, when the LORD said to me, 'Assemble the people to Me, that I may let them hear My words so they may learn to fear Me all the days they live on the earth, and that they may teach their children.' You came near and stood at the foot of the mountain, and the mountain burned with fire to the very heart of the heavens: darkness, cloud, and thick gloom. Then the LORD spoke to you from the midst of the fire; you heard the sound of words, but you saw no form—only a voice."

(DEUTERONOMY 4:5–12 NASB)

The darkness that accompanies You should not fabricate weakness in us, but strength. It should not birth fear, but courage. It should not bring about fleeing, but hearts that are prepared to stand and receive.

We fall on our faces before You, and you bring with Your presence restoration for the purpose of revelation.

What connection is there between keeping statutes and judgments and giving heed to oneself in order to keep one's soul diligently? The former seems to point to the Law that stands as a reminder of sin. The latter seems to point to the broken and contrite heart which the Lord our God will not despise. We have seen the manifestation of the Lord's glory, and those manifestations, once settled, will not be able to depart from one's heart. Thus, they must be settled. The settling occurs only when we come near. The settling occurs when we stand at the foot of the mountain. The settling occurs as the mountain burns with fire, and we do not run from the advancing flames; rather, we hold with the knowledge that the flames will come so far and no farther. The line that divides us from holiness's flames is, before the Father, the line of Messianic Advocacy. The settling occurs as we do not shrink back from the darkness, the cloud, the thick gloom, but instead we become familiar with it. So familiar, that darkness's cloud of thick gloom becomes my neighbor whom I welcome with bread, and milk, and fattened calf. We learn to sit and rest with one another awhile. Then a fire does not rage. Instead, the fire dances, it warms, it welcomes. The fire is friend, and I am a friend of God. From the flames Friendship speaks. As one once said, the One from Whom the voice comes, "Is not safe, but most certainly is good."

There is no need to be afraid of the dark or the flames that accompany the darkness, for, from inside, the sweet voice of Friendship speaks.

I do not need to see His form because His form is the span that once measured out my very existence and His hand which has authored the perfect story of my life. He Who formed me, and Who has authored all of my days, before there is yet one of them, calls me to welcome His Authorship, even when the Author appears with darkness.

Darkness IV

Then Solomon assembled the elders of Israel and all the heads of the tribes, the leaders of the fathers' households of the sons of Israel, to King Solomon in Jerusalem, to bring up the ark of the covenant of the LORD from the city of David, which is Zion. All the men of Israel assembled themselves to King Solomon at the feast, in the month Ethanim, which is the seventh month. Then all the elders of Israel came, and the priests took up the ark. They brought up the ark of the LORD and the tent of meeting and all the holy utensils, which were in the tent, and the priests and the Levites brought them up. And King Solomon and all the congregation of Israel, who were assembled to him, were with him before the ark, sacrificing so many sheep and oxen they could not be counted or numbered. Then the priests brought the ark of the covenant of the LORD to its place, into the inner sanctuary of the house, to the most holy place, under the wings of the cherubim. For the cherubim spread their wings over the place of the ark, and the cherubim made a covering over the ark and its poles from above. But the poles were so long that the ends of the poles could be seen from the holy place before the inner sanctuary, but they could not be seen outside; they are there to this day. There was nothing in the ark except the two tablets of stone which Moses put there at Horeb, where the LORD made a covenant with the sons of Israel, when they came out of the land of Egypt. It happened that when the priests came from the holy place, the cloud filled the house of the LORD, so that the priests could not stand to minister because of the cloud, for the glory of the LORD filled the house of the LORD.

Then Solomon said,

"The LORD has said that He would dwell in the thick cloud.

"I have surely built You a lofty house,

"A place for Your dwelling forever."

(1 KINGS 8:1–13 NASB)

For the choir director. A Psalm of David the servant of the LORD, who spoke to the LORD the words of this song in the day that the LORD delivered him from the hand of all his enemies and from the hand of Saul.

And he said,
"I love You, O LORD, my strength."
The LORD is my rock and my fortress and my deliverer,
My God, my rock, in whom I take refuge;
My shield and the horn of my salvation, my stronghold.
I call upon the LORD, who is worthy to be praised,
And I am saved from my enemies.

The cords of death encompassed me,
And the torrents of ungodliness terrified me.
The cords of Sheol surrounded me;
The snares of death confronted me.
In my distress I called upon the LORD,
And cried to my God for help;
He heard my voice out of His temple,
And my cry for help before Him came into His ears.

Then the earth shook and quaked;
And the foundations of the mountains were trembling
And were shaken, because He was angry.
Smoke went up out of His nostrils,
And fire from His mouth devoured;
Coals were kindled by it.
He bowed the heavens also, and came down
With thick darkness under His feet.
He rode upon a cherub and flew;
And He sped upon the wings of the wind.
He made darkness His hiding place, His canopy around Him,
Darkness of waters, thick clouds of the skies.

From the brightness before Him passed His thick clouds,
Hailstones and coals of fire.
The LORD also thundered in the heavens,
And the Most High uttered His voice,
Hailstones and coals of fire.
He sent out His arrows, and scattered them,
And lightning flashes in abundance, and routed them.
Then the channels of water appeared,
And the foundations of the world were laid bare
At Your rebuke, O LORD,
At the blast of the breath of Your nostrils.

He sent from on high, He took me;
He drew me out of many waters.
He delivered me from my strong enemy,
And from those who hated me, for they were too mighty for me.
They confronted me in the day of my calamity,
But the LORD was my stay.
He brought me forth also into a broad place;
He rescued me, because He delighted in me.

(PSALM 18:1–19 NASB)

God dwells in the thick darkness of a cloud. If there is no need for sun and moon in God's heaven, then there must be sufficient light. Before we reach His radiance, through what darkness must each pass? How wide, how long, how far a journey through the thickest mists that stand as the foundation for His revelatory presence must be traversed?

Their actions were honorable. Their actions were righteous. For years upon years, in the tent of a sojourner, the Lord met them in movement. They built according to God's exact specifications. They had been showered with Egypt's riches; now Egypt's riches had been sanctified, no longer theirs, if they ever had been at all. God's cattle from thousands of hills stand even more glorious than the gold of the Nile. They constructed, and sewed, and forged, and fashioned, and assembled, and erected, and then His darkness plunged.

When He descended, they stood and worshiped.

When He ascended, they tore down, covered up, set out, and followed.

When He stopped, the process began all over again.

Now, no more moving.

Now, no more tearing down.

Now, there would be permanence. Yet, God has never dwelt in the houses of creation but the hearts of humanity. Now or then, why should anything be any different? A house allows us to stop. A house allows us to appoint God, rather than God appointing us. A house can be one of our personal design and declaration, selfishly saying, "See what I have created for You, God. See what I have created for You."

We become settled. We begin to dictate. We start to design and assume the role of Creator, rather than acknowledge our nature as creation. None is ever to be our place or our position. So, once again, the dark cloud settles in and drives us from Spirit and true worship of God.

All the blood of bulls and goats, far too many to number, mean nothing. The Word of God remains inside, but nothing else. Is it an indication of neglect or necessity? Certainly, He Who speaks from darkness's midst will decide and declare. No matter how loud we cry out saying, "I have surely built You a lofty house, a place for Your dwelling forever," darkness seems to be a more fitting residence for the Creator of the universe. God's grace and declaration of truth is all that resides in our self-constructed palaces of brick and stone. It is we who are created to dwell in the House of the Lord forever. His construct for us, not our construct for Him.

May we always prefer the darkness of God's cloud to the sanctuary of humanity's design.

Solomon's father teaches all too well the lesson that declares our God is a Rock and not a god who falsely dwells within them. God takes stones, sprinkles clean water upon them, and they are made clean. They become flesh, and God dwells within them. We are God's people. He is our God.

The darkness of death that attempts to hold God's children simply generates anger, and movement, and salvation from the One Who has made our hearts flesh. Cords, and torrents, and snares wrapping about God's children, simply actuate the Lord's nostrils. They flare, and, with a divine snort, darkness and fire appear. God is not the dragon of old. God is good, the only good, and the Shepherd's angry snarl does not kill, steal, or destroy. His snarl properly positions. That which is dead releases and returns to its place of death. That which has been made alive and is loved by the Father is released and saved from the enemy.

God hears the voice of His children, just as His children know the voice of their Father. As a hen gathers chicks, so the voice of the Gatherer's distressed children moves the Great and Mighty Parent to action, where, against the dark safety of Parent's breast, we once again lie. Once again, our deliverance to safety calls us to both nurse and be weaned.

How large must the cherub be that is saddled and ridden by the Lord of the universe?

The thunder and lightning of this world is but a pop and a flash to the weather of Creator, but it is enough. The Lord's might has rolled in, and we are saved. He sent. We have been taken. We have been both drawn and delivered. The road to God may be narrow, but that is only because the surrendered enter one at a time. The home of God's children is eternally spacious.

The darkness of death has ended.

The darkness of salvation surrounds us.

Whom shall we fear?

There are none.

So comes the dawn.

Jesus' trial

They led Jesus away to the high priest; and all the chief priests and the elders and the scribes gathered together. Peter had followed Him at a distance, right into the courtyard of the high priest; and he was sitting with the officers and warming himself at the fire. Now the chief priests and the whole Council kept trying to obtain testimony against Jesus to put Him to death, and they were not finding any. For many were giving false testimony against Him, but their testimony was not consistent. Some stood up and began to give false testimony against Him, saying, "We heard Him say, 'I will destroy this temple made with hands, and in three days I will build another made without hands.'" Not even in this respect was their testimony consistent. The high priest stood up and came forward and questioned Jesus, saying, "Do You not answer? What is it that these men are testifying against You?" But He kept silent and did not answer. Again the high priest was questioning Him, and saying to Him, "Are You the Christ, the Son of the Blessed One?" And Jesus said, "I am; and you shall see THE SON OF MAN SITTING AT THE RIGHT HAND OF POWER, and COMING WITH THE CLOUDS OF HEAVEN." Tearing his clothes, the high priest said, "What further need do we have of witnesses? You have heard the blasphemy; how does it seem to you?" And they all condemned Him to be deserving of death. Some began to spit at Him, and to blindfold Him, and to beat Him with their fists, and to say to Him, "Prophesy!" And the officers received Him with slaps in the face.

(MARK 14:53–65 NASB)

"It has begun. So be it."

Mary spoke these words three years prior as her Son turned water to wine and resolutely set His face in the direction of His awaiting Jerusalem cross and borrowed tomb.

A borrowed tomb: Like Jonah before Him, there was no need for a permanent one because He would only, for three days, be borrowing.

Messiah's calling.

Father's will.

Divine timetable.

With the trial that is no trial, it begins again. Perhaps it is just the culmination.

The sheep now lead Ezekiel's Shepherd to the courtroom of the slaughter. This unholy convocation was not the great cloud of witnesses, nor the community of the to-be-martyred. This assembling was for tearing down the One Who had come to rescue and edify. Like Babel before, those gathered did their very best to cry out with one voice, but instead, as they built their institution unto themselves, their speech was confusion and not communion. Human structures began to unravel, and dispersion seemed to be their lot; that is until the Christ appeared in their midst, and He testified with His voice that both harmonizes His siblings and divides competitive humanity. The One Who could have united them, they seized. They rejectingly rallied around division, and their fists struck the One Who had come to bring them life more abundant.

The world has woken up. All around us, I hear its slams that announce mechanization has dawned for another day. The world does not wait until the sun rises. It is awake by creation's own choice and design. Against the backdrop of our striving that has ceased, in order that we would know that He is God, we can hear Babylon roar.

There is Temple construction directed by God. There is temple construction directed by humanity. Those He has come to rescue do not know He will be torn down in six hours. Yet, after the Friday sands descend the glass, is the One Who framed and fashioned the universe's sands with His words and humanity with the sands able to reconstruct, in but three days, the virgin-born, but now destroyed Temple?

He answered, "Yes." He testified, "I am the Master Builder."

They said, "We have no more need for witnesses." And the razing of the Temple began.

It began with spittle.

It began with blows.

It began with a blindfold.

It began with mocking.

It began with a bag of silver and a torn robe.

And, now, they taunted Him with chants, crying, "Prophesy!"

When will creation ever listen to her Creator? Two did not originally. Most did not then. Most do not now. Most will not tomorrow. But there will always be a remnant.

There was a Seth, and there was an Enoch. There was a Noah, and there was an Abram. There was an Isaac, and there was a Jacob. There was a Joseph, and there was a Judah. There was a Moses, and there was a Joshua. There was a Samuel, and there was a David. There was a Daniel, and a Nehemiah, and an Ezra, and prophets. There was a silence, and there was a Zacharias and Elizabeth. There was His mother, and there was a Joseph. There was a Voice in the wilderness, and there were two. There were twelve, and there were seventy. There were a few at the roots of a manmade tree of execution, and a Joseph of Arimathea, along with a Nicodemus, who were granted permission to take His body down from the tree. There were those whose hearts were burning within them, and there were children who still could catch no fish. There were one hundred and twenty, and there is a Bride. We are all sheep, and because our Shepherd is the One Who was led as a lamb to the slaughter and opened not His mouth, among us today, we hear and know His voice. We listen. Even in the midst of our failures, we listen.

We wait, and we listen.

We look to the east of His return, and we listen.

Soon He will call, and the listening will be received.

Come Lord Jesus, come.

Peter's three-time denial

Simon Peter was following Jesus, and so was another disciple. Now that disciple was known to the high priest, and entered with Jesus into the court of the high priest, but Peter was standing at the door outside. So the other disciple, who was known to the high priest, went out and spoke to the doorkeeper, and brought Peter in. Then the slave-girl who kept the door said to Peter, "You are not also one of this man's disciples, are you?" He said, "I am not." Now the slaves and the officers were standing there, having made a charcoal fire, for it was cold and they were warming themselves; and Peter was also with them, standing and warming himself.

The high priest then questioned Jesus about His disciples, and about His teaching. Jesus answered him, "I have spoken openly to the world; I always taught in synagogues and in the temple, where all the Jews come together; and I spoke nothing in secret. Why do you question Me? Question those who have heard what I spoke to them; they know what I said." When He had said this, one of the officers standing nearby struck Jesus, saying, "Is that the way You answer the high priest?" Jesus answered him, "If I have spoken wrongly, testify of the wrong; but if rightly, why do you strike Me?" So Annas sent Him bound to Caiaphas the high priest.

Now Simon Peter was standing and warming himself. So they said to him, "You are not also one of His disciples, are you?" He denied it, and said, "I am not." One of the slaves of the high priest, being a relative of the one whose ear Peter cut off, said, "Did I not see you in the garden with Him?" Peter then denied it again, and immediately a rooster crowed.

(John 18:15–27 NASB)

The Lord turned and looked at Peter. And Peter remembered the word of the Lord, how He had told him, "Before a rooster crows today, you will deny Me three times." And he went out and wept bitterly.

(LUKE 22:61, 62 NASB)

We should be fascinated by the denial at the door and the meeting of the eyes.

John knew the girl who kept the door to the High Priest's courtyard. John speaks to her to permit Peter access to Jesus' place of holding. Peter had been warned he would be sifted as wheat. He was told he was going to deny. He was reprimanded for sleeping. He was reprimanded for violence. He had run away, rather than lay down his life for the Imprisoned. This is a bold one's shot at redemption.

Redemption is a tenuous word.

John says to Peter, "Hold tight, and I'll see what I can do."

Peter agrees and waits.

And waits.

And waits.

"Come on, *Pete*. She'll let you through."

He moves toward the door within earshot of his friend.

"So, you're one of them too, are you?"

"I am not. I do not know the man."

Fascinating, but his denial is also fitting. Even within the sphere of influence of one we claim to influence, sometimes we can be the denier.

One, two, three denials, and then comes a powerful moment. Less than a second after denial number three drips from Peter's lips, his eyes rise to a pair of eyes already looking compassionately upon him. Peter had told Jesus he would be the one who would save Jesus, not deny Jesus. It was Peter who was against going to Jerusalem altogether and against all this crazy talk about Jesus' death. Peter had told the Door to the sheepfold that if anything was going to come against Him, then they would have to go through him. Once, twice, thrice the hireling fled. And now there is a meeting of the eyes. The eyes of one who claimed to be His savior meet the eyes of the One Who is his Savior.

The cock crows.

All out of fight, with bitter tears painting the ground, Peter flies away.

"The Lord turned and looked at Peter. And Peter remembered the word of the Lord, how He had told him, 'Before a rooster crows today, you will deny Me three times.' And he went out and wept bitterly."

(LUKE 22:61, 62 NASB)

How could he have forgotten? It is always the look that calls us to remember. How easily we forget, but Peter is not alone. Everyone there had heard His teachings in the synagogues and in the Temple, and just like Peter, they too had forgotten. In the direction of them all, Jesus surveyed, but in His direction, they chose not to gaze. Conviction of the world by the One has a tendency to cause others to forget—conveniently or otherwise.

I have forgotten and been called to remember.

You have forgotten and been called to remember.

He looks to the eyes of us all.

Our gaze must not fly to the darkness but must fall before the atmosphere of the Rescuer's light.

Judas

Now when morning came, all the chief priests and the elders of the people conferred together against Jesus to put Him to death; and they bound Him, and led Him away and delivered Him to Pilate the governor.

Then when Judas, who had betrayed Him, saw that He had been condemned, he felt remorse and returned the thirty pieces of silver to the chief priests and elders, saying, "I have sinned by betraying innocent blood." But they said, "What is that to us? See to that yourself!" And he threw the pieces of silver into the temple sanctuary and departed; and he went away and hanged himself. The chief priests took the pieces of silver and said, "It is not lawful to put them into the temple treasury, since it is the price of blood." And they conferred together and with the money bought the Potter's Field as a burial place for strangers. For this reason that field has been called the Field of Blood to this day. Then that which was spoken through Jeremiah the prophet was fulfilled: "AND THEY TOOK THE THIRTY PIECES OF SILVER, THE PRICE OF THE ONE WHOSE PRICE HAD BEEN SET by the sons of Israel; AND THEY GAVE THEM FOR THE POTTER'S FIELD, AS THE LORD DIRECTED ME."

(*MATTHEW 27:1–10 NASB*)

There is a feeling of sickness. Innocence pursues us, but is our tendency to run away from readied spiritual salvage? Judas is blamed, but he certainly is not distinct. Still, the finger always seems to conveniently, with great judgment, point to Judas. He is not to be celebrated. He is not to be vilified. He is himself just as we are ourselves. That night, he lived one of the lives of betrayal.

Each has done so.

Each is loved.

Each boy and girl has been extended the younger son's opportunity to return. The Father watches and waits with robe, ring, and fatted calf ready. It is the older brother that condemns Judas. It is the older brother that condemns each. It is the older brother who condemns both those in the city and those closest to home. Judas squandered. Each has squandered. Even those who have remained all along, and received everything, see their reception as nothing but duty, and they wait for a young-goat-worthy approval. Such is their squandering.

Who is the guilty one? Who is the innocent one? Who is the one who receives a wine-soaked piece of bread into his mouth from the hands of the soon-to-be-betrayed Savior? All of us do. In *his* betrayal, Judas is distinct. In distinction, *all* have betrayed.

God is Righteous Judge.

Jesus before Pilate

Then they led Jesus from Caiaphas into the Praetorium, and it was early; and they themselves did not enter into the Praetorium so that they would not be defiled, but might eat the Passover. Therefore, Pilate went out to them and said, "What accusation do you bring against this Man?" They answered and said to him, "If this Man were not an evildoer, we would not have delivered Him to you." So Pilate said to them, "Take Him yourselves, and judge Him according to your law." The Jews said to him, "We are not permitted to put anyone to death," to fulfill the word of Jesus which He spoke, signifying by what kind of death He was about to die.

Therefore, Pilate entered again into the Praetorium, and summoned Jesus and said to Him, "Are You the King of the Jews?" Jesus answered, "Are you saying this on your own initiative, or did others tell you about Me?" Pilate answered, "I am not a Jew, am I? Your own nation and the chief priests delivered You to me; what have You done?" Jesus answered, "My kingdom is not of this world. If My kingdom were of this world, then My servants would be fighting so that I would not be handed over to the Jews; but as it is, My kingdom is not of this realm." Therefore, Pilate said to Him, "So You are a king?" Jesus answered, "You say correctly that I am a king. For this I have been born, and for this I have come into the world, to testify to the truth. Everyone who is of the truth hears My voice." Pilate said to Him, "What is truth?" And when he had said this, he went out again to the Jews and said to them, "I find no guilt in Him."

(JOHN 18:28–38 NASB)

That all those would know Your voice, O God.

"My kingdom is not of this world."
"My kingdom is not of this world."
"My kingdom is not of this world."

This is the place our present day finds itself. Jesus' kingdom is not of this world. So, there is a decision to be made: His kingdom or the kingdom of this world?

Jesus lived a life of surrender to His holy nature and remained in His holy atmosphere. No matter the external unholy conditions, Jesus never compromises His holy nature by moving from His atmosphere. Ultimately, Jesus' example must become our reality. As we surrender to Jesus' holy nature inside of us, our internal nature and external atmosphere are characterized by the fruit of the Spirit: *love, joy, peace, patience, kindness, goodness, faithfulness, gentleness, self-control.* Jesus' authority is derived from a very different order of things. The King's voice sings of His kingdom.

That all those would know Your voice, O God.

Jesus before Herod

Then Pilate said to the chief priests and the crowds, "I find no guilt in this man." But they kept on insisting, saying, "He stirs up the people, teaching all over Judea, starting from Galilee even as far as this place."

When Pilate heard it, he asked whether the man was a Galilean. And when he learned that He belonged to Herod's jurisdiction, he sent Him to Herod, who himself also was in Jerusalem at that time.

Now Herod was very glad when he saw Jesus, for he had wanted to see Him for a long time, because he had been hearing about Him and was hoping to see some sign performed by Him. And he questioned Him at some length; but He answered him nothing. And the chief priests and the scribes were standing there, accusing Him vehemently. And Herod with his soldiers, after treating Him with contempt and mocking Him, dressed Him in a gorgeous robe and sent Him back to Pilate.

(LUKE 23:4–11 NASB)

The Pharisees look at Herod's kingdom with contempt.

Jesus has no interest in the Pharisees' or Herod's kingdom, but He gazes upon its subjects with compassion and a desire to deliver. Herod is part of the same hypocrisy as Pilate's kingdom ... and the kingdom of religious institutionalism ... and every fool's kingdom. Kingdoms such as these seek after profitability and the miraculous. Profit and miracles provide Babel-like stability to the kingdoms of bureaucratic advancement, both religious and secular.

Such kingdoms are not our homes. We are not slaves to the two-coins-tax for me and thee but to the One Who has seen that the tribute would be held between Pisces' lips. We do not serve God in convenience, nor in fairness of weather. Holiday is not our call to attendance but evidence of our rhythm. We do not seek a sign. We serve humanity as bondservants of the Savior, Jesus Christ the Lord.

He has received a crown of thorns, so we seek not a crown of roses.

To the kingdoms of this world we say, "Adorn us with His robe. Place His staff of ridicule in our hands. Jeer and jest as you did to our Lord. We are the bruised for Christ. We are His smoldering wicks.

"We will not be broken by you but for Him. We will not be snuffed out for anything but the cause of Christ. We desire to lose our lives that they would be saved."

Which bar-Abba?

Now at the feast, the governor was accustomed to release for the people any one prisoner whom they wanted. At that time, they were holding a notorious prisoner, called Barabbas. So when the people gathered together, Pilate said to them, "Whom do you want me to release for you? Barabbas, or Jesus who is called Christ?" For he knew that because of envy they had handed Him over.

While he was sitting on the judgment seat, his wife sent him a message, saying, "Have nothing to do with that righteous Man; for last night I suffered greatly in a dream because of Him." But the chief priests and the elders persuaded the crowds to ask for Barabbas and to put Jesus to death. But the governor said to them, "Which of the two do you want me to release for you?" And they said, "Barabbas." Pilate said to them, "Then what shall I do with Jesus who is called Christ?" They all said, "Crucify Him!" And he said, "Why, what evil has He done?" But they kept shouting all the more, saying, "Crucify Him!"

(MATTHEW 27:15–23 NASB)

Who is the fool?

Who is the one ruled by his stomach?

Who is the one ruled by lust and consumption and violence?

We do not serve a God of convenience or appetite.

We cry for bar-Abba, when, among us, is *From the Father*, God with us.

Beaten, mocked, and rejected, *From the Father* looks at bar-Abba and weeps. The Shepherd has never turned from His *to-seek-and-save-the-lost words* that compassionately instruct His siblings, saying, *"Blessed are those who mourn, for they shall be comforted."* (Matthew 5:4 NASB)

From the Father weeps for the one between the two who offers the choice, and for the one the mob will choose. *From the Father* mourns for those who, with frenzied song, sing, "Away with *From the Father!* We want bar-Abba!" *From the Father* cries for His mother, and the women, and John. Through their tears, they are the only ones who cast their vote, saying, *"From the Father."*

He who has offered the choice returns to them bar-Abba, and, settled in His mourning, *From the Father* submissively waits for comfort.

Scourging

He went out again to the Jews and said to them, "I find no guilt in Him. But you have a custom that I release someone for you at the Passover; do you wish then that I release for you the King of the Jews?" So they cried out again, saying, "Not this Man, but Barabbas." Now Barabbas was a robber.

Pilate then took Jesus and scourged Him. And the soldiers twisted together a crown of thorns and put it on His head, and put a purple robe on Him; and they began to come up to Him and say, "Hail, King of the Jews!" and to give Him slaps in the face.

(John 18:38–19:3 NASB)

Exhaustion begins to overwhelm. When we wait through the night with expectation of resurrection, then there is restoration and hope. Yet this dawn gives us neither restoration nor hope. This dawn gives us denial, judgment, cries for bar-Abba, and scourging to come. This dawn brings us His pain, His journey, His passion, His death. It will be over soon.

But not yet.

I am so tired, Lord, but not as tired as You were. Your pain is not mine to bear. You are the one that journeyed the gauntlet and set the captives free. In the midst of your passion, Lord, wash me with Your strength.

May I forever serve with bravery for the Christ whose stripes have made me free.

Spirit calls me to press on and survive the darkness of which He so clearly introduced me to throughout the night. Strange how the greatness of darkness appears with the dawn. Some of us know this all too well.

How many towels are needed to absorb the Savior's blood? The tool for absorption is not a towel but the surrendered heart. Graciously enough, the surrendered heart can absorb it all.

As for Him, the wings of Spirit hover over me and renew my strength.

Pilate's judgment

When Pilate saw that he was accomplishing nothing, but rather that a riot was starting, he took water and washed his hands in front of the crowd, saying, "I am innocent of this Man's blood; see to that yourselves." And all the people said, "His blood shall be on us and on our children!" Then he released Barabbas for them; but after having Jesus scourged, he handed Him over to be crucified.

(MATTHEW 27:24–26 NASB)

How much water is necessary to wash the blood of the Messiah from one's hands? There is not enough. We are to be washed and regenerated by Holy Spirit. He sprinkles clean water upon us, and we shall be clean. We are to be born of water and the Spirit.

Repentance and new birth.

The waters of repentance.

The blood of new birth.

He was judged, and yet He did not come into the world to judge the world. He came to love and to heal and to save. All one act, as we will surrender to it.

We have judged ourselves by the place of our belief's stance.

"His blood shall be on us and on our children!"

O, that it only were. And yet, it is on us and all our children, one way or the other.

We are judged, and His blood is on our guilty hands.

We are judged, and our guilty hearts receive His bloodied hands.

One is the judgment of death.

One is the judgment of life.

Only the water made wine washes us clean from our guilt.

"This beginning of His signs Jesus did in Cana of Galilee, and He manifested His glory, and His disciples believed in Him."

(JOHN 2:11 NASB)

Via Dolorosa

And following Him was a large crowd of the people, and of women who were mourning and lamenting Him. But Jesus turning to them said, "Daughters of Jerusalem, stop weeping for Me, but weep for yourselves and for your children. For behold, the days are coming when they will say, 'Blessed are the barren, and the wombs that never bore, and the breasts that never nursed.' Then they will begin TO SAY TO THE MOUNTAINS, 'FALL ON US,' AND TO THE HILLS, 'COVER US.' For if they do these things when the tree is green, what will happen when it is dry?"

Two others also, who were criminals, were being led away to be put to death with Him.

(LUKE 23:27–32 NASB)

As He begins to walk toward a home that was not His own, some are on their faces, some are rising from their knees, some are still kneeling upon them. All in this room are broken in realization of the cross He embraces, the cross He welcomes, the cross He carries to usher in our rescue.

The world does not understand His embrace of the growing-more-bloodied wood. They call Him a fool for doing so, but His wisdom has always been foolishness to them, and their wisdom is equally contrary to Him and His siblings.

How long is this journey?

The hour declared in prayer, has now, most certainly, come.

It is an hour seen even before Eden, but in the dust-filled garden-of-perfection, its clarity is discernible. It is an hour alive in Abel's assassination and in the marking of his failed keeper. It is an hour noticeable in Lamech's murderous seventy times seven, as much as it is beheld in its forgiving counterpart. It is an hour reflected in each moment of the ark's construction; and in Noah's compassion that infused every second, of every minute, of every hour, of every day, of every week, of every month, for more than a year while, beneath them, floated the foreshadowing of death's drowning.

The hour of all things made new is present in Abram's dark night, and it is visible in Isaac's first sight of his bride. It is seen when Jacob refuses to let go and when Joseph refuses to return evil for evil. The hour is seen over four hundred years of slavery and sojourning. The hour is seen when Moses returns. The hour is seen in ten plagues and a Red Sea crossing. The hour is seen as rebellious Egypt dies and readied Israel lives. The hour is seen when Hebrew wilderness wanderers, over and again, take life for granted. The hour is seen when Michael allows the Lord to contend with Satan. The hour is seen when God speaks to Joshua saying, "Be strong and courageous, for as I stood with Moses, so I now stand with you." The hour is seen when Joshua offers the choice. The hour is seen when the judges rule, Eli fails, and Samuel is supplanted by a king who resembles all the other nations.

The hour is seen when they don't reject him, but they reject You.

The hour is seen in David's anointing and in David's adultery. The hour is seen when God declares exile. The hour is seen when Daniel confesses, Nehemiah prays, and Ezra stands and reads for hours. The hour is seen when, at the digging of the footers, children-become-elders weep. The hour is seen when Gabriel brings message, and message, and message again. The hour is seen when the mute one now speaks and says, "And you my child ..." The hour is seen when they travel 120 miles to fulfill the prophecy of God while they register for the world. The hour is seen at His circumcision, and His dedication, and the prophecy over Him, and Simeon and Anna's consolation of finally going home. The hour is seen in the losing, and the finding, and the teaching, and the correcting, and the submitting, and the growing in stature and wisdom with God and man. The hour is seen when the voice begins crying in the wilderness and baptizing with water. The hour is seen when it is let it be so for now, the Spirit descends, the Father speaks, and Elijah testifies, saying, "Behold the

Lamb of God that takes away the sins of the world." The hour is seen when they ask Him where He is staying. The hour is seen with every "Come and see." The hour is seen as He teaches in their synagogues, and their Temple, and their fields, and their homes. The hour is seen in "Who touched me?" The hour is seen in "Talitha koum." The hour is seen in "I condemn you neither. Go and sin no more." The hour is seen in "Lazarus, come out." The hour is seen in "Leave her alone. She has prepared Me for My burial." The hour is seen in the bread and in the cup. The hour is seen as they sing a hymn and go out into the night. The hour is seen as He prays to the Father, "Father, the hour has come; glorify Your Son, that the Son may glorify You ..."

The hour of His crucifixion has nearly come.

This cross is the final passageway to the reception of the keys of death and Hades.

His hour has reconciled all of our hours.

Simon's change of heart

They pressed into service a passer-by coming from the country, Simon of Cyrene (the father of Alexander and Rufus), to bear His cross. Then they brought Him to the place Golgotha, which is trans-lated, Place of a Skull.

(Mark 15:21, 22 NASB)

Without his sons, while holding the Son, he says ...
"Almost there.
"We're nearly there."

The one who made sure they knew he was innocent, now looks into the eyes of the One he once believed was guilty. As he does, this one with-out his sons embraces his guilt and declares the Son's innocence.

He is now free to go. But, with one last look, he gathers himself in the eyes of the One worthy to be free but Who joyfully welcomes the cup.

In all of us, Thy will be done.

From all of us, the tears are flowing more freely. May they continue to flow until the time of our celebration of resurrection. We welcome the dark cloud of Your emerging presence, so that we would see Your grave of soli-tude, and the fire of Your glorious resurrection.

Glory to Your Name.

Amen and Amen!

Crucifixion

*It was the third hour when they crucified Him. The inscription of
the charge against Him read, "THE KING OF THE JEWS."*

(MARK 15:25, 26 NASB)

What do we know of death? As much as the Lord reveals to us. As much as we know, God knows more. As we stand at His death, He meets us with compassion.

The history must be told again.

God stood next to Adam and Eve as they first died.

God held Able as he slipped away.

God watched with Noah as Divine tears flooded the earth and brought forth creation's death.

God walked Mount Moriah much longer and farther than Abraham and Isaac ever had to walk.

God carried Esau and Jacob from murderous dishonesty and slavery to stomachs, to the place of submission and service. God witnessed selfishness die and their brotherhood live eternally.

As the world told Jacob his Joseph was dead, God told Him to look to Egypt, for there Israel would see not death but life.

Moses said, "I will die in their place." Though he did not enter in, God's hands placed His friend Moses's body in the ground.

"Joshua, Moses is dead. Be strong and courageous, for as I was with Moses, so I now stand with you."

God received Jephthah's daughter and David's son. They will not return to us, but we will return to them.

You, O God, cried with Your mother as she buried her uncle, her aunt, and her husband.

You, O God, were broken over Your cousin, Your baptizer.

With a hand on his coffin, You gave him back to the widow at Nain.

You, O God, wept at Lazarus' tomb, and then received him into Your bosom as he took his last steps from this world.

Every death there ever was; every death there is; every death to come, God stands beside and mourns. God mourns that we welcomed death into His gift of perfection. He died and delivered us to life ... a life sojourning amidst existence and expiration.

Death is no more.

Live.

Thieves on flanking crosses

One of the criminals who were hanged there was hurling abuse at Him, saying, "Are You not the Christ? Save Yourself and us!" But the other answered and, rebuking him, said, "Do you not even fear God, since you are under the same sentence of condemnation? And we indeed are suffering justly, for we are receiving what we deserve for our deeds; but this man has done nothing wrong." And he was saying, "Jesus, remember me when You come in Your kingdom!" And He said to him, "Truly I say to you, today you shall be with Me in Paradise."

(LUKE 23:39–43 NASB)

The day begins with both criminals hurling insults toward Jesus, but somewhere along the way or upon the crosses, with one of the criminals a change of heart occurs. Did he see Jesus' innocence, or was he made aware of his own guilt, or was it an equal descent to both? To find guilt among guilt is not difficult. The kingdom of guilt naturally produces recognizable defiance, resulting in destruction of community and the trampling of love. Both of those flanking Him, while wanting to justify themselves, assumed Jesus' guilt. No matter the instability of our self-justification, we believe, if we can point to the guilt of others, then perhaps our own innocence can be fabricated. The death of a martyr or a patriot is far more stomach-able than that of a criminal. A crucified Jesus must be guilty. Yet how had these men never heard of the One Who so freely pronounced His messianic ordination?

Again, the kingdoms of this world have no fraternization with the rule and reign of God. Not every piece of produce from bad trees of the era knew to climb the sycamore because Jesus was on His way. He did not eat at the table of every tree house. Even those walking to Emmaus, and Miss Mary of Magdalene, weeping in the garden, failed to recognize the Christ before them, though they knew Him intimately.

So, with that, assumption of guilt, fabrication of innocence, and messianic ignorance are the ingredients for their hurled abuses.

Somewhere a heart gets broken, a soul is convicted, and defense for the Other, rather than the one, begins to be formed. Certainly, as the pain, suffocation, and exhaustion grows, the insults will be more easily offered. Yet would he possess both the courage to speak out for His innocence and the vulnerability to acknowledge their guilt? With his final bits of strength, it would be far easier to die with a gasp than to offer vindication for Another.

The time comes within three hours.

Sometime between the 9:00 a.m. crucifixion and the sky darkening at noon, more insults are birthed. This time, the One receiving the insults continues to do so quietly, but the ridiculing duet has now become a solo because one-half of the guilty duo refuses to sing along.

"Sing, you fool. I have sung my part, now you must sing yours ... I said, sing!"

"But I don't want to sing any longer ... not ... at least ... that song."

"You sang it well this morning!"

"But I have come to know it is no longer a true song. In my self-justification, I believed it to be, but in the presence of perfect innocence, I find myself not only no longer justified, but also entirely guilty ... and so are you. This man ... He is the innocent One."

It is a familiar song Satan sings. It was a tune offered with measured poise three years prior. In the Jerusalem amphitheater of the Temple's pinnacle, Satan sang, "If You are Who You say You are, then come down and declare Who You are, supposed Son of Man." One was a long leap without nails; the other was a short step with nails. Jesus did not perform.

Jesus is no actor.

The Messiah is no exhibitionist.

Christ is not the incarnate troubadour of a divine troupe.

Savior is no jester waiting for the applause that actuate encore.

Jesus is the suffering servant, Who, from the place of no greater love, lays down His life for His friends. Anyone can come. There is no admission, just open seating. Disciple is welcome. Whore is welcome. Eunuch is welcome. Two criminals on either side are welcome. At the place of the skull, only one chooses to attend. He requests admittance into His kingdom.

Jesus dismisses his begging and continues to die beside him as the two together prepare to step into the glory of paradise.

Leave the song.

Receive the Lyrical Poet Who sings you as His poem while dying beside you.

In the midst of a nearly dark afternoon, morning has broken.

Middle-of-the-day darkness

It was now about the sixth hour, and darkness fell over the whole land until the ninth hour, because the sun was obscured; and the veil of the temple was torn in two.

(Luke 23:44, 45 NASB)

The time to write has come again. Preparations are made for darkness because it is nearly noon. I am so very tired, yet I cannot imagine the weight of the Savior's exhaustion. My eyes burn, my mind swims, my body aches, but in comparison to the burden of the Lord's crucified state, I am everlastingly whole. Soon we enter the final steps of darkness's last descent into glory.

The Messiah's hands are stretched with fingers spread.

The Messiah's head bows low. He is hair draped without face.

He hangs in place while legs spasm.

He melts into the pools of early death, but it won't be long. His toes already bathe in the grave.

Spirit, as at His baptism, hovers over Him as a Dove.

What was it that obscured the sun? Was it the horde of sin? Loneliness perhaps was sun's covering. Did Savior face enough pain to blacken moon's counterpart?

My mind is stale.

The inspiration is spent.

Perhaps the darkness can be necessary restoration.

We exit by the same road through which we entered.

He leads us out.

Shrouded in shadows did they sit and wait?

Sitting.

Waiting.

I have watched for movement. I have watched for the chest to rise and fall. I have counted the seconds between the last ... and the next ... breaths. It transitions from seconds, to minutes, to wondering if there will be another. Little is said, and comfort is no help to stem the tide of waiting for death to arrive. Still, our Christ should not have died so soon. Somehow they must have known. Somehow we all know, or at least we can offer a sufficient list of what He must have been carrying for the gate of death to swing wide.

We know our own portion.

The rest most likely cannot, nor should not be imagined, for it was reality and not imagination at all.

Did they swarm Him in an attempt to drive Him insane?

Did they, within the moment, call Him to find a solitary place of comfort, and peace, and hope, and then, deep into an already agitated wound, trickle a salty drop of sweat?

They could beat Him no more. There was no more need for additional nails. How much of His agony is separated from their active participation? His body would fill and swell, struggle and deplete. That which His body needed for survival was slipping away. That which perpetuated His death came in physiological waves. They stood by and cheered. There was no need for them to advance the physically deteriorating agenda.

Did they get so caught up in His dying that they failed to see that His death precipitated their defeat? No one who loves Jesus wants Jesus to die, but with a broken heart, they faithfully welcome gracious release. But no Elohim enemy who knew of Jesus' Lordship should have hungered for Golgotha. The Savior is fixed. The surrendered One, in dying, is winning. Enemy is nearer to the rich man's side of the chasm than is the crucified Messiah.

We wait.

We watch and wait.

If something away from the darkness occupies my thoughts, am I sinning? Do I begin to care less? Can I even see an Occupier within the dark cloud?

Does He look at me, consider me, does He still minister as Messiah? He prayed that we would be forgiven, but as He petitions Father's throne for the strength to soon cry out, "It is finished!" does He look heavenward or toward me?

Who remains?

Is there a pause in the admonition to focus upon willing spirit over weakened flesh, or is His charge all the stronger? It was far simpler when He was speaking of sleep rather than my personal declaration of His Lordship.

Here, it is noisy as people attempt to settle. Had the darkness stilled Calvary's mountain?

It is still two hours before the Lamb dies on this throne of crossed wood and then never again. For those who understand the sacrifice, repetition will be no more.

Be still.

In communion with Christ, the longer one spends in the darkness, the lighter the darkness becomes.

We must locate the God Who is resurrected. We are about to celebrate His resurrection, but where is He? Do we even know? I understand He is in the commonplace and in our conversations, but apart from the miraculous among us, where is the manifestation of His presence? I speak of His peace. I speak of His love. I speak of community. I speak of sacrificial giving with no desire for return. I speak of tongues that are neither conjurings nor products of indoctrination. I speak of revolution that has no desire to redeem the world's systems but an uprising of deliverance for the lost and lingering. I speak of crying being strength and holding back tears being repression. I speak of grieving as those who possess hope. I speak of prayer with few words and no drawn attention to oneself. I speak of the balance of faithfulness and fellowship, where holiness is upheld, and without compromising the character of the One True God, a universal welcome is extended.

How alone was our Lord?

One-half hour remains.

God, thank You that my words can be stated, and You allow them to rest before You. I am committed to You creating a place here where You will be, and where individuals will be invited to engage with You. Hopefully, many will do so, and we will become community; and, from community, the community will be invited to share in a purity without compromise. We are not interested in simple experience. We simply desire You—just a sharing in and of You. And as we meet with You, we join with one another. My prejudice must be burned up. My judgment must cease to exist. I must only offer invitation and relationship—invitation to Your presence; relationship with You and one another.

We will pray.

We will feed on Your Scriptures.

We will fast.

We will worship.

We will compassionately minister.

This darkness has compelled me. This darkness has revealed my perfections. This darkness has revealed my imperfections. I offer my heart. I offer my love. I am transparent before You.

The death of Jesus

Therefore, the soldiers did these things. But standing by the cross of Jesus were His mother, and His mother's sister, Mary the wife of Clopas, and Mary Magdalene. When Jesus then saw His mother, and the disciple whom He loved, standing nearby, He said to His mother, "Woman, behold your son!" Then He said to the disciple, "Behold your mother!" From that hour the disciple took her into his own household.

After this, Jesus, knowing that all things had already been accomplished to fulfill the Scripture, said, "I am thirsty." A jar full of sour wine was standing there; so they put a sponge full of the sour wine upon a branch of hyssop and brought it up to His mouth. Therefore, when Jesus had received the sour wine, He said, "It is finished!" And He bowed His head and gave up His spirit.

(JOHN 19:25–30 NASB)

And behold, the veil of the temple was torn in two from top to bottom ...

(MATTHEW 27:51A. NASB)

Then the Jews, because it was the day of preparation, so that the bodies would not remain on the cross on the Sabbath (for that Sabbath was a high day), asked Pilate that their legs might be broken, and that they might be taken away. So the soldiers came, and broke the legs of the first man and of the other who was crucified with Him; but coming to Jesus, when they saw that He was already dead, they did not break His legs. But one of the soldiers pierced His side with a spear, and immediately blood and water came out. And he who has seen has testified, and his testimony is true; and he knows that he is telling the truth, so that you also may believe. For these things came to pass to fulfill the Scripture, "NOT A BONE

OF HIM SHALL BE BROKEN." And again another Scripture says,
"THEY SHALL LOOK ON HIM WHOM THEY PIERCED."

(JOHN 19:31–37 NASB)

These are the last moments of His body's passion existence. These are the moments before victory came. The Messiah never quit. He pressed on to accomplishment, and humanity's rescue was insured.

A mother had a son.

A son had a mother.

Satan shrieked in eternal loss. Certainly, creation would be tormented and creation would groan, but the opportunity for Abba-breathed life lives before us all with the pall of sin to one day be removed through the fires of new creation. There will be new heaven and new earth.

The veil has been rent from top to bottom, and while the Tree of Life is not yet to be taken from, a new Tree of Salvation grows beside it and bids us to eat through submission until the Messiah returns on the Eastern clouds.

There is much work to do, Lord Jesus, but I cry out, "Come, Lord Jesus, come!"

Glory be to You, our perfect sacrifice.

More silence and darkness

I have been awake now for twenty-four hours. Each year our God grants me rest at this time, and rest I will. As I do, I pray God burns the judgment from my heart, the unrighteous anger from my heart, the older brother spirit from within me. When I awake, as the sun sets, I pray that dawn has arisen and compassion is growing inside of me.

I have walked the journey of crucifixion once again. I am honored and prepared to celebrate the resurrection of our Lord.

God of all.

Friday, April 14, 2017, 6:23 p.m.

God granted me sweet sleep for two hours, and I am refreshed. While I cannot say the older brother is dead within me, he certainly is silent. Hopefully, he will move from my life soon. I no longer want to condescend. I would rather descend.

This time has taught me that I must descend into vigil. I must descend into worship. I must descend into the Eucharist. I must descend into the presentation of my feet and the washing of the feet of others. I must descend into solitude and a minimal community. I must descend into the divine darkness that always precedes the flames of God's glory. I must descend into Gethsemane and Christ's agony there. I must descend into Judas' kiss, and Peter's violence, and the Messiah's submission. I must descend into the Sheep being led to the slaughter. I must descend into the back-and-forth of Good Friday's morning. I must descend into the scourging, the crown, the reed, and the robe. I must descend into the insults of two thieves that transform into the insults of one and the recognized necessary petitions of the other. I must descend into 9:00 a.m. crucifixion, and noontime darkness, and 3:00 p.m. cries. Into the six hours of Friday, there must be descent. I must descend into the release of

His mother. I must descend into the release of His beloved. They are one another's now. I must descend into the fullness of Psalm 22, not simply its beginning, nor only its end. I must descend into the request for His body. I must descend into the hearts of Joseph and Nicodemus. I must descend into the Garden Tomb.

I must descend.

Until Sunday comes, and then we will all rise together in His Life.

We prepare to worship as we look to the glory of cracked stone. My brother, Jason sings, "Those who fear the grave never find the truth."

And so this journey to resurrection culminates.

Death is not extinguishing the light
but merely putting out the lamp
because the dawn has come.

—Rabindranath Tagore

Worship and waiting for the resurrected Lord

This is a time where we worship, and we wait. Many in this world are stripping their churches. It is an appropriate stripping and one welcomed by our crucified Lord. Yet the tradition of this assembly is to worship and wait for the resurrected Lord. We have walked His crucifixion, so now, we worship and we wait.

Christians are a knowing people.

We know that our Lord is alive. He is not here; He is risen. Paraclete is with us, but He is not here. He is risen, and He is ascended, and He is seated to the right, and He is advocating for those connected and those who are still clinging, and He is coming again—perhaps not today, but maybe. Still, today, while we wait ... we worship. He is our God alone.

Thank You, Lord.
Thank You.
We say it to You again and again.

Two friends, old friends, praying together. They will be best pals forever.

My family in the front row.

My family in the back row.

My family in every seat throughout the room.

Who is my mother, and my brothers, and my sisters? Those who do the will of my Father in heaven are both my mother, and my brothers, and my sisters.

Those words are appropriately spoken by every son and daughter of the living God. If He is our Brother, then she is just as well our mother and our sister. We have but one Father who is in heaven. We are all siblings, together. His anointing is upon us.

The cross is the chain that I am to cast off one day. The chain of His suffering will be exchanged for a crown. It is a crown laid up for me, and not only for me, but also for all of those who have loved His appearing.

There is a woman who is crying who I did not expect to cry. May my expectation ever be being created fresh.

Hands go up, and hands go out. People stand.

They stand to receive.

Such is worship and reception of the Creator Who creates us.

The humility of her wisdom astounds me. If wisdom is a woman, then she embodies her.

There is no masquerade here. As they come to know one another intimately, they will dance this dance of worship more beautifully together.

The barefoot troubadours.

They follow the Spirit, but soon the set list will be no more. No longer will they possess a modicum of measure. Spirit is fashioning them. Extra is going. Insufficiency is either eliminated or edified. It is only for His glory. Every song becomes a hymn of "Thank You!"

Thirty-six hours has become less than twelve.

Nearly everyone looks heavenward to the glory of the King of kings. It is the primary posture of prayer. With eyes wide open, we see Him high and lifted up.

What does it mean that His name is power, breath and living water? How does His name shape marred clay? How does the saying of the name, Immanuel, burn up wood, hay, and stubble, and make already precious stones even more precious?

Such a marvelous mystery.

No longer servants, we simply meet with You, God.

While it is fine to have closed eyes, swaying forms, and lifted hands, it is just as well to sit back and enjoy Him and the worshipper's love for God. A *soul-let-go* is just as beautiful—just as courageously vulnerable. He may speak those words to the tides, but God never says to us, "This far you may come but no farther. Here you must stop." God calls us deeper and deeper still. It is the woman who has seen and experienced so much, who sings, "It is well with my soul. I trust in You, God," as flesh of her flesh stands in worship, and her gift sings, "Through it all, through it all my eyes are on you."

You know every person I am speaking of, for each is just as much a part of your community as each is of mine. The same hurts, the same fears, the same pains, the same present troubles, the same joys and celebrations, we are certainly one family. He is our Abba. We say to Him, "Dad." How wonderful that we know we have but one Father, and the one Father allows us to have so many we can call "Dad."

We must learn the environment of worship. It can be Sabbath, but it can also be *everyday*. Perhaps it would be best to start with *everyday* before we attempt to receive the gift of Sabbath. Sabbath cannot be Sabbath until every day of *everyday* is spent in communion with God. From lying down, to sweet sleep, to rising up, to going along the way, to the return home, to lying down again. Every moment with God, every moment with man, every moment must be God ordained and done as unto the glory of God. The moment of celebration is easily settled into. The moment of desperation is then the next step. While more difficult, we still cry out for His comfort. So celebration and desperation are both experiences where the presence of God is more easily welcomed. It is the normalcy of days that rocks us to sleep from His ordination and creating among us. Once we settle there, then we begin to learn worship's environment. Worship is celebratory. Worship is desperation. Yet worship is also normalcy. Everyday normalcy is daily manna, not miraculous increase. Everyday normalcy is water from a long-standing well with vessel with which to draw, and it is not drought that pleads. Normalcy has nothing to do with event, and yet, sometimes normalcy finds its occurrence there. Celebration, desperation, and normalcy, such are the moments of worship alive every day.

A wicked and adulterous people solely seek after events of celebration. A wicked and adulterous people struggle to sing in desperation. God's people properly approach them all. God's people, within the normalcy of every day, celebrate their desperation alongside the gracious God, and so, they simply worship God and receive all these things God desires to add to them.

Then Sabbath comes.

It is a day of deeper perfection that exists within already perfect communion and relationship. It was present in Eden and most likely was practiced. We have no idea how long they were there before the cycle of separation was initiated and made complete. Then came separation. Then came birth pains. Then came desire for and ruling over. Then came thistles, and thorns, and resistance. Then came association with dust. These must be perfected within the reality of their never-changing or never-change-able mutation, and then we can settle into Sabbath. Sabbath is a gift, so separation must be served to a place of communion with God and neigh-bor. Sabbath is a gift, so we are to see pain as perfection. Sabbath is a gift, so *desire-for* must become a *desire-to* love even when no love is returned. Sabbath is a gift, so ruling over must be transformed into serving rather than being served and giving our lives as a ransom for many. Sabbath is a gift, so the strength of thistles, and thorns, and resistance must be respected and then authoritatively removed from the places where God desires good soil. We must never be ashamed to stand in God's authority where rebellious creation tries to stand its ground. Sabbath is a gift, so God's redeemed are no longer dust but spirit and truth. Eden is just as alive today as then, but unlike then, now a storm swirls at her borders. Remain in Eden, living the perfection of communion and relationship, and then we will begin to step into the gift of Sabbath. We must learn the mastery of service, and communion, and relationship within the six days, or else we will never carry the seventh back to them. If we do not carry the seventh day back to the six, then the six will never know the salvation of the seventh.

Such are the six.

Such is the Sabbath.

All can be a gift once again.

It is not an easy thing to worship God every moment of every day. We desire the respite of the world rather than the peace of His silence. We must learn the peace of His silence as our choice, rather than naturally fleeing to the false consolation of the world. It cannot console us, and it is not neighbor. Resting in the peace of His silence after spirit and truth worship is a learned behavior that must flow naturally from our relationship with Spirit and Truth.

It is the greatest of blessings to hear the Trinity sing through the three.

You do comfort us during the waiting, Lord.

Nothing contrived. Nothing orchestrated. They just worship You. They no longer are repeating in song the lyrics of others. Now they sing their songs to the Lord. They struggle a bit, like a child first begins steps ... but Spirit keeps singing through them. You hold their hands. They stumble underneath Your holding, but they do not fall.

Blessed assurance,
Jesus is yours ... and mine.

Worship to midnight

With overflowing praise, God's prophetic word over His children must be accompanied. The Tribe of Judah leads us into His courts with glorifying exaltation. There alone do we hear His words. To Him they are not prophecy because He knows no yesterday, today, or tomorrow. *I Am* simply is. So, without moment or moments, the word of *Is* flows forth. A cry out should no longer startle. Now, it simply calls within the *I Am*. For it, *I Am* has called.

And so we wait.

And so we listen.

There is a fluttering among us because there is a fluttering over us. Holy Spirit rests upon us and flutters at the edge of our ears. It is not the wings of angels but God *Is-self*. What will this night become except morning? There is but one revelation, and Spirit, our Teacher calls us to sweep away the dust from its edges to reveal the revelatory intricacies.

Operate in Me.

Live in Me.

Spirit says.

Candles no longer holding man's oil still burn brightly despite oil's absence. What will this night become except the fires of God's glory? I sit, but Spirit calls me to sit even lower. I know not why. Perhaps this is the descent where I will meet God in the deeper still. I thought condemnation would reign down here, but it does not. His cleansing is alive at the place of the floor. One of my heroes joins me here. Will there be others? Certainly, others are listening.

The greatest intimacy is to be found upon the soles of the feet. No wonder He calls us to take time to wash them. In washing, we are washed. Is it fatigue or fluttering that calls me to lie down?

It is so much easier when God takes my hand to write each sentence.

I lie down, face up on the floor.

The fluttering calls me to this season of joy. Spirit calls me to open my mouth as *Is* exhales. Holy breath drives the impurities away from my deep within. The breath breathed in the Garden is now breathed afresh in me.

The humility of being found.

God says ...

Lie down and actuate the courage of vulnerability. They may meet you there, and if not, you will be ever-calling them to do so. Soon they will be there. Soon they will arrive. Just be patient, My son, for I am with you, and I am leading them. There is no need to be afraid. I have made your mouth. Just continue to speak My words, and everything will be okay.

Jacob's Dream—my dear brother's voice comforts me and so many others.

How far I have traveled with You, my God. Many years we have walked, and talked, and waited, and worked together. All of the days have brought us to this day—this day which is preparing to be the next. Three days that are one. Thirty-six hours of three blessed days become one. I will never forget them, Lord. Typically, not so many are here, but tonight there are certainly some among us. I'm honored that they are listening to Your servants, God. Listening to Your servants, my friends, the brotherhood of the silence.

Open up my eyes in wonder.

Midnight to dawn worship

Saturday, April 15, 2017, Midnight

My dear brother has sung of taking, and blessing, and breaking, and sending. We are so very honored to be all. Our God has reached out to us and stripped us from the scales that covered us. There is a blessing as we are washed. The gold that strangles our arm is broken, as is our heart, and we begin to love Him, so that we may be sent. There is nothing that binds us any longer. No shackles keep us in. We are free, and now the One calls us to be created within the freedom of God's presence. God is before and behind. God is beside and over. God is firm foundation. God surrounds us and keeps us in with a freedom that allows us to go in and out and find pasture. It is God Who sustains us. These are things that are known and have been taught, and yet, each-day-manna's presence as the dew before us calls us to eat from God's provision alone. Not too much is to be taken. Not too little is to be gathered. Our God is just right. When His holiness fills the temple that I am and you are, it is both enough to undo us and then immediately cleanse and call us. Even when they will not listen, we remain His mouth, and His feet, and His arms with which to embrace a tear-streaked world that cries out while still holding on to what is dying.

Blessed are those who mourn. Mourn over sin. It is not in our presence that they do these things. If it were, then righteous anger would be appropriate. But no ... they do in their worlds as they search for being. His surrounding protects us, so as we move from the Manger to the Inn, we do so to call them to gather with those who naturally grunt and groan, rather than those who do so outside of the confines of the Creator's fashioning hands. They must stop rebelling against the Creator as they claim divinity and identify with the dust.

It is dark again.

Night has dawned once more.

Tonight, I'm no longer afraid of the dark.

Yet, I stand as a dad desiring for a son to be delivered from his seizures.

Will the One Who has descended from transfiguration's mountain heal, or will He calmly ask me how long he has been this way?

Simply initiate Your healing, Lord.

The crowd is coming. So, now He heals.

Isn't it interesting how God pauses just long enough to make us accept a certainty that He just might not, and then I will remain in the hold of seizures forever? Then, before me, there is no more seizing.

The silence is nearly over. There will be only one more moment of it before Morning Prayer. Brother has sung, and brother sings. Sister will soon sing, and then perhaps brother again, and then there will be silence. Holy Spirit has established His place. He will not move, unless there is dramatic shift in us, but I can sense and see Spirit is settling in for a time of less movement. Spirit needs no rest, but before our weekend celebration of Savior's resurrection, He settles in.

The Third Person of the Trinity calls me to the Scriptures.

Meditation of silence

The most difficult and fulfilling moments of our year have almost reached their final places of silence. I struggle to even find the keystrokes of my desire.

What must it have been like for them? They will tell us one day ... maybe. They thought they were making preparations for the Passover, and certainly they thought the possibility could be possible, but never did they think it would be probable. The chance for the leaders lying in wait in Jerusalem to kill Him was certainly a reality, but would He allow them? They had tried so many times before with stones, and cliffs, and arrests, but none ever came to fruition. Why would He allow it this time? They had heard Him say that He had the authority to lay down His life and take it up again. This would be like every other Passover before. There would be confrontation, but He would speak boldly and survive again. They would be back in Galilee within two weeks. All would be well.

But not this time.

This time He would lay His life down in order to take it up again.

Their celebration that would be feast, and sacrifice, and feast, and celebration, and wine, and laughter, and rest, and return home would not be so this time.

Now, sleep had left them. They woke Thursday to Jesus' call for preparations, and other than the hour where they *could, but would not tarry* while in Gethsemane, no sleep had come to them. In anguish they were awake. In disappointment they were awake. In fear they were awake. Their bodies hurt and so did their hearts.

Our Saturday holds knowledge, and our Sunday holds celebration, but in the conformity of *their minds*, Sabbath and Sunday held only death.

Death of their Rabbi.

Perhaps death of themselves.

They were more quiet than we presently are.

I just stepped outside to walk our youngest worship leader to her car. I grew up with her dad, and I respect him too much to allow his daughter to walk in the darkness to her car by herself. My fear of darkness may have been squelched the last thirty-four hours, but that has not eliminated the danger darkness possesses.

As we stepped outside, I called the one who has sung so beautifully for the Lord, the one who has allowed us to listen in, to listen herself. Moon nearly full and a clear sky seemed to say night, but it is no longer. The two of us listened and the birds were declaring the dawn. They always do. Even before mechanization hums, the ravens, and the sparrows, and the robins tell us it is morning. They sing even before the cock crows. The old rooster has crowed enough. He stands as the enemy's tool of great accusation. We need him no longer. With resurrection and ascension, now it is Spirit Who convicts the world of sin, and righteousness, and judgment. His conviction is the deepest depth of holiness, and honesty, and honest darkness, but He possesses no accusation. Spirit's conviction comes with hope and a clearly marked way.

He is our guiding hand.

The worship we experienced for ten hours was pure. Jesus told the one with no husband that the Father is Spirit and He is Truth, and He is searching for those of spirit and truth to worship Him. The Messiah said we have arrived in the epoch when it is not where one worships, but how. For ten hours from Friday night to Saturday morning, mercy preceded sacrifice, and our Spirit and Truth God gladly welcomed both. He sang, and she sang, and she sang, and he sang, and they sang. No one was jockeying. They all just played, and surrendered, and sang, and treated us to the opening of God's Throne Room's doors.

Seven men are here. Six are in the sanctuary, and one is resting outside our makeshift Upper Room. It held a greater aesthetic thirty-four and a half hours ago. Now it is no more than our entryway once again. We are nearly back again to the familiar. A man of God who has lived strength's perfection has lit a candle and now walks from row to row and chair to chair praying for children who will be here soon. They will sit in their seats with their parents listening to the gospel.

His death.

His burial.

His resurrection.

He is Jesus.

And Jesus is fulfillment of the Messiah's good news.

I know him well. He will pass by soon and kiss me on top of my head.

The Messiah has already kissed me, even though I also kissed Him. I stand amazed at His forgiveness. We speak of it so very much ... His forgiveness. The One Who needed none carries it in His womb, and to whosoever will extend hands, His womb freely births forgiveness' matured gestation.

The kiss has arrived.

This vigil has been so much more than survival. In years past, we were well intentioned, but it became more of either a show or an endurance event. Make no mistake, it has always been approached with reverence, and it has always been edifying, but as our surrender to God's creating hand grows, so grows the depth of our relationship with the Godhead as we walk this Holy Week journey with God.

One candle remains shining among the twelve stationed on the platform.

One at the cross.

One on the platform.

The one at the cross would probably say he did far less than shine.

I begin to think that maybe my writing is breaking this time of final silence. Not for others but for myself. They cannot hear my fingers tapping the keys, but my mind is speaking through keystrokes far more than my spirit is presently listening for the voice of Good Shepherd.

So silence should be silent.

Prayer will begin soon.

God's peace and God's blessings be upon you.

Morning has broken

For the choir director. A Psalm of David.
In You, O LORD, I have taken refuge;
Let me never be ashamed;
In Your righteousness deliver me.
Incline Your ear to me, rescue me quickly;
Be to me a rock of strength,
A stronghold to save me.
For You are my rock and my fortress;
For Your name's sake You will lead me and guide me.
You will pull me out of the net which they have secretly laid for me,
For You are my strength.
Into Your hand I commit my spirit;
You have ransomed me, O LORD, God of truth.

I hate those who regard vain idols,
But I trust in the LORD.
I will rejoice and be glad in Your lovingkindness,
Because You have seen my affliction;
You have known the troubles of my soul,
And You have not given me over into the hand of the enemy;
You have set my feet in a large place.

Be gracious to me, O LORD, for I am in distress;
My eye is wasted away from grief, my soul and my body also.
For my life is spent with sorrow
And my years with sighing;
My strength has failed because of my iniquity,
And my body has wasted away.
Because of all my adversaries, I have become a reproach,
Especially to my neighbors,
And an object of dread to my acquaintances;

Those who see me in the street flee from me.
I am forgotten as a dead man, out of mind;
I am like a broken vessel.
For I have heard the slander of many,
Terror is on every side;
While they took counsel together against me,
They schemed to take away my life.

But as for me, I trust in You, O LORD,
I say, "You are my God."
My times are in Your hand;
Deliver me from the hand of my enemies and from those who
    persecute me.
Make Your face to shine upon Your servant;
Save me with Your lovingkindness.
Let me not be put to shame, O LORD, for I call upon You;
Let the wicked be put to shame, let them be silent in Sheol.
Let the lying lips be mute,
Which speak arrogantly against the righteous
With pride and contempt.

How great is Your goodness,
Which You have stored up for those who fear You,
Which You have wrought for those who take refuge in You,
Before the sons of men!
You hide them in the secret place of Your presence from the
    conspiracies of man;
You keep them secretly in a shelter from the strife of tongues.
Blessed be the LORD,
For He has made marvelous His lovingkindness to me in a
    besieged city.
As for me, I said in my alarm,
"I am cut off from before Your eyes";

Nevertheless, You heard the voice of my supplications
When I cried to You.

O love the LORD, all you His godly ones!
The LORD preserves the faithful
And fully recompenses the proud doer.
Be strong and let your heart take courage,
All you who hope in the LORD.

(PSALM 31 NASB)

"Man, who is born of woman,
Is short-lived and full of turmoil.
"Like a flower he comes forth and withers.
He also flees like a shadow and does not remain.
"You also open Your eyes on him
And bring him into judgment with Yourself.
"Who can make the clean out of the unclean?
No one!
"Since his days are determined,
The number of his months is with You;
And his limits You have set so that he cannot pass.
"Turn Your gaze from him that he may rest,
Until he fulfills his day like a hired man.

"For there is hope for a tree,
When it is cut down, that it will sprout again,
And its shoots will not fail.
"Though its roots grow old in the ground
And its stump dies in the dry soil,
At the scent of water it will flourish
And put forth sprigs like a plant.
"But man dies and lies prostrate.
Man expires, and where is he?

"As water evaporates from the sea,
And a river becomes parched and dried up,
So man lies down and does not rise.
Until the heavens are no longer,
He will not awake nor be aroused out of his sleep.

"Oh that You would hide me in Sheol,
That You would conceal me until Your wrath returns to You,
That You would set a limit for me and remember me!
"If a man dies, will he live again?
All the days of my struggle I will wait
Until my change comes."

(JOB 14:1–14 NASB)

After these things, Joseph of Arimathea, being a disciple of Jesus,
but a secret one for fear of the Jews, asked Pilate that he might take
away the body of Jesus; and Pilate granted permission. So he came
and took away His body. Nicodemus, who had first come to Him by
night, also came, bringing a mixture of myrrh and aloes, about a
hundred pounds weight. So they took the body of Jesus and bound
it in linen wrappings with the spices, as is the burial custom of the
Jews. Now in the place where He was crucified there was a garden,
and in the garden a new tomb in which no one had yet been laid.
Therefore, because of the Jewish day of preparation, since the tomb
was nearby, they laid Jesus there.

(JOHN 19:38–42 NASB)

Both David and Job have been blessed. Both David and Job are now broken before the Lord, and the ridicule of men has done anything but salved their wounds. David cries out to God. Job cries out to no one in particular. Maybe the considered man speaks to his chastisers, maybe to the God with Whom he once had sweet fellowship, but in his grief, Job simply bemoans to the air surrounding him. David's complaints are always salted with praise, but here Job sees little hope except in the hope that God may only "hide Job in the grave and conceal him till God's anger has passed!" Job desires for God to "set a time for Job and then remember him." Until then, Job would just rather God keep His distance and allow Job to wallow in the boils ravaging his body, coupled with the ridicule from those who were once friends that ravages his ears.

Job speaks a truth that is common to both his and David's mindset: Who can bring what is pure from the impure? No one! Job sees the fallacy of humanity. David sees it too. The Messiah died for both the hopeless and the hopeful who cry out for the fact and the fallacy. Does Joseph of Arimathea stand as Job, preferring to be hidden until God's appointed time to call him? Perhaps that is why he remained as a cloaked disciple of the Galilean. While under the cloud of the crucifixion, is Nicodemus offering a David-like offering to God? Was more than a hundred pounds of aloes and spices necessary to prepare one body, even if it were the body of the One Who claimed to be Messiah, but Who now seems to be more a possessor of death than a giver of life?

On this day of knowing-waiting, we look to the celebration of the resurrected Messiah. Jesus resurrects from the Garden Tomb to bring salvation to every Job whose grief creates in him a desire to just be left alone until the time to be gathered to his people. Jesus brings salvation to every David who, within the same Psalms, both complains and praises. Jesus brings salvation to every Joseph who has the courage to request the body of Jesus from our Roman procurators but the cowardice that prohibits a public stand beside the One he claims to be Messiah. Jesus brings salvation to every Nicodemus who dutifully surrenders an overabundant and unnecessary tithe that will be obsolete when Jesus ceases to be dead rabbi, but Who proves Himself to be the three-day reconstructed Temple, Who is greater than the Temple soon to be razed.

What are our offerings? Good riddance is a bad offering. A mixture of complaints and praises is not sweet aroma but sour taste. Requesting and then hiding is a moth-eaten purse. Too much when enough will do is overkill. Still, Jesus meets Job at the place of his cries, David in his swaying, Joseph in his cowardice, and Nicodemus in his excess. He meets each of us too and offers us rescue from sin and death.

To each of us, God is speaking the words spoken through the prophet Nathan to King David, saying, "The LORD also has taken away your sin; you shall not die" (2 Samuel 12:13 NASB). To each of us, God has extended these pronouncements of grace: *"Adonai also has taken away your sin. You will not die."* This is the good news of the Messiah's gospel. The realization of Jesus' unified death, burial, and resurrection has established rescue for all those bound by sin and death, and all are bound. Amazingly, all have sinned, are sinning, and will sin, but those surrendered and submitted to this good news live in the declaration of sin's removal. How many people are bound by the fear of death—both their own physical expiration and the grief and loneliness potentially present in the passing of loved ones? Jesus, with great hope, counters, saying, "But I say to you truthfully, there are some of those standing here who will not taste death until they see the kingdom of God" (Luke 9:27 NASB). Jesus is not talking about sinful, spiritually dead people reaching out, taking from the Tree of Life, eating, and living forever apart from communion with the Godhead. Jesus recognizes our deteriorating biology, and He calls us, while present within it, to release physiology, and with both hands, cling to the one life that cannot die. This is not make-believe. While sojourning in a world of sin and death, all have been granted access to a reality of holiness and eternal life. If you choose to accept it, Adonai has taken away your sin; and you will not die.

Glory be to our risen King.

A concluding wait for what we know to be true

I once heard, "You cannot fully experience the resurrection until you have fully experienced the crucifixion." I believe we have not *done* our very best to *do* so this year; rather, this year, we allowed God to create us.

God created our ...

Well ... God simply created, and simple is never simpler.

Death no longer has victory.

Death no longer has sting.

Our Jesus is alive ... forever.

An Interlude of Invitation to Bear the Christ Who Bears Our Wounds

Before the next *RSVP* or *regret* is rendered, a few final questions. Have you now stumbled over the messianic leaf? Will you cease all battles against the One Who has journeyed to rescue? Will you humbly descend and surrender to being found? As an act of gratitude, will you walk your rescued journey alongside the rescuing journey of the Messiah's death, burial, and resurrection? Will you submissively live the rest of your days carrying out your only remaining responsibility:

bearing the Christ Who bears our wounds?

You are now cordially invited ...

BEARING THE CHRIST WHO BEARS OUR WOUNDS

BEARING THE CHRIST
WHO BEARS OUR WOUNDS

"... and lo, I am with you always, even to the end of the age."

(MATTHEW 28:20B NASB)

No one in Christendom will argue against Jesus' ascension, but as the Messiah offers the above Great Commission promise, neither should anyone deny Jesus' presence among us. From fifty days beyond the pre-crucifixion Passover, the Spirit of the Messiah has been with us. Thus, I propose a new mindset: Because Christ came to us and is still with us, let's stop asking Christ to re-enter a world in which He already exists to smooth out our troubles and prohibit our deaths and instead bring ourselves, our troubles, our circumstances, our sicknesses, our pains, our mortality to the Savior Who has already overcome all these things. In Jesus' beatings, humiliation, death, burial, and resurrection, every sickness, death, and disease has been defeated, so each must remove his/her hands from the wounds the Messiah has already received and overcome. We are only responsible for bearing the Messiah Who bears our wounds.

While we will always be in the throes of sickness, disease, hardship, and death, the Messiah has provided an exit from the full force of their destructive effects. As it pertains to sickness, disease, and hardship, Isaiah prophesies, saying, "Surely our griefs He Himself bore, and our sorrows

He carried; yet we ourselves esteemed Him stricken, smitten of God, and afflicted. But He was pierced through for our transgressions, He was crushed for our iniquities; the chastening for our well-being fell upon Him, and by His scourging we are healed" (Isaiah 53:4, 5 NASB). And, as to death, Paul counsels Timothy, saying, "But now has been revealed by the appearing of our Savior Christ Jesus, Who abolished death and brought life and immortality to light through the Gospel" (2 Timothy 1:10 NASB).

Isaiah writes during a time when both Assyrian and Babylonian enemies are bearing down upon Israel's Northern and Southern Kingdoms. And Paul is suffering in prison as a result of his gospel ministry, when he pens his words to Timothy. While waiting in unfavorable conditions for the Messiah's ultimate return, neither Paul nor Isaiah would ever deny pain and death. Only a blind fool does such a thing. Still, contrastingly, both point to freedom, and life, and, dare we say, immortality as the dominant conditions declaring victory. Both, from their own frames of reference, say the Messiah, through beatings, humiliation, death, burial, and resurrection, has forever defeated every sickness, death, and disease; and now, available to all through messianic portal, are freedom, life, and immortality. Eternal calls to Everlasting and says, "While this world's winds will howl until your flesh is blown away by them, you, Everlasting, never have to leave Eternal Immortality's hand again." This is the promise all have messianic access to while living in this buffeting world.

The forces of sickness, hardship, injustice, and mortality possess great power to divert our focus from the Messiah's victory over such things. But we must remember, while each is still present until the end of the age, they are defeated foes. How do we access victory while living in such a present dichotomy? Four examples of exit are offered.

As a child, I stayed over at my grandmother's many a summer evening. There were two conditions that proved to be unfavorable to my getting a good night's sleep: Granny's house did not have air-conditioning, and I was a restless little boy. My saving grace came in my grandmother who was a counselor and a purveyor of peace. In that hot upstairs bedroom, I would thrash about in an attempt to cast the heat from me. All my restlessness was accomplishing was an even greater generation of heat. Granny would place her gentle hand on my back, quietly speak words of peace, and I would begin to be very still. Somehow, some way, amidst the heat, Granny called me to the untroubled cool of slumber. I learned at a very early age heat's effects were alive and well, but I did not have to give in to their powers.

In the fourth chapter of his gospel, John Mark records the account of a calmed storm. His testimony says Jesus, one evening, suggested to His disciples that they go over to the other side of the Sea of Galilee. Who were they to argue with the beginning-to-be-believed-to-be Messiah, so they followed His lead, got in the boat, and headed to the other side of the lake. There were many seasoned fishermen among the band of merry men, so when Jesus fell asleep in the stern there was no cause for alarm. Jesus was a fine rabbi, but the jury was still out as to the Nazarene's sea-worthiness. Then, all of a sudden, a storm arose with a force strong enough to kill all of them. Mark reports there was great panic, and their open fishing boat was already filling with water. As they were looking down the barrel of their final sea-faring days, where was Jesus? The Teacher was still sleeping on a cushion. It prompts the question: If a storm is so powerful that it can bring panic and the knowledge of impending death to old-school fishermen, then how could a Teacher of the Torah be at such peace He could remain asleep in a boat filling with water? They wake up Jesus. They reprimand Jesus for sleeping and beg Jesus to use His power, saying, "Save yourself and us!" Jesus says "Shhhhhh" to the winds and the waves. Then the Messiah turns to His disciples and questions them, saying, "Why are you so afraid? Do you still have no faith?" (Mark 4:40 NASB) The Rabbi Savior's lesson rings true then and now: Even amid panic and death-bringing storms, it is wiser to peacefully lie down next to the sleeping Savior and His declaration of a completed journey to the other side.

No parent should ever have to bury her child. Jesus' mother had to do so. And long before Sunday's resurrection, Mary had to watch her Son be beaten, humiliated, deserted by nearly all His friends, unjustly sentenced,

paraded through the streets of Jerusalem, and be mocked while hanging in disgraced and death-bringing crucifixion. Mary's pain was real,
and the mother of the Lord had only an over-the-horizon idea of her
Son's potential resurrection. Bearing such pain, resurrected life was not
on her mind. Michelangelo's *Pietà* reflects Mary's pain as she holds her
Son's wound-riddled corpse. Yet in the great artist's sculpture, there is
an even greater message. Jesus Messiah's death, burial, and resurrection
initiated a new reality. No longer is anyone responsible for carrying her
own wounds, sicknesses, diseases, or mortality. The wounds and death of
her Son Mary was carrying no longer had to be carried by her. Yes, Mary
had to weather the three-day gospel storm, but Michelangelo's sculpture's
greatest declaration is this: Mary had to hold her Son and not the wounds
her Son was holding. While receiving pain, and deterioration, and death,
all are welcomed to only hold the Christ because the Christ holds all for
us. He does not need our assistance. He only desires us to receive His
healing grace.

Jesus says to Thomas, "Reach here with your finger, and see My
hands; and reach here your hand and put it into My side; and do not be
unbelieving, but believing" (John 20:27 NASB). Jesus said these words
to Thomas, not only so Thomas would believe Jesus' resurrection. Jesus
also wanted Thomas and all those in attendance to understand the
wounds He bore were both His and theirs. Isaiah's prophetic words had
been fulfilled. Jesus Messiah is the One Who, "[Bore our griefs], and our
sorrows He carried; yet we ourselves esteemed Him stricken, smitten of
God, and afflicted. But He was pierced through for our transgressions,
He was crushed for our iniquities; the chastening for our well-being fell
upon Him, and by His scourging we are healed" (Isaiah 53:4, 5 NASB). As
Thomas touches the wounds of Jesus, Jesus declares to all creation we are
no longer responsible for carrying wounds, sickness, decay, injustice, and
mortality. The resurrected Messiah has forever taken this responsibility.
We are only responsible for holding Christ and not our wounds and death
the Christ has defeated and bears.

Heat must acknowledge its defeat when each surrenders to stillness of a gentle hand and the cool of slumber.

Storms can either rage on or still themselves when each chooses to lie down next to the sleeping, faithful Christ.

And be you a mother or a friend, you are no longer responsible for bearing your own wounds, but only the Messiah Who bears them.